Aunt Alice's Goodies

✦

Old Time Recipes We Grew Up With

Alice Stevens

iUniverse, Inc.
New York   Bloomington

Aunt Alice's Goodies
Old Time Recipes We Grew Up With

Copyright © 2008 by Alice Stevens

iUniverse books may be ordered through booksellers or by contacting:

iUniverse
1663 Liberty Drive
Bloomington, IN 47403
www.iuniverse.com
1-800-Authors (1-800-288-4677)

ISBN: 978-0-595-52689-5 (pbk)
ISBN: 978-0-595-62743-1 (ebk)

Printed in the United States of America

For Christopher and Emily

and all the

Allgaier cousins

Contents

Miscellaneous Goodies

Introduction

Welcome to *Aunt Alice's Goodies*. I am aunt Alice. Over the years from my hippie beginnings in the late 1960s, through my politically active 1970s, on into single motherhood and the financially wild eighties, including my cancer-ridden 1990s, and moving along into the turn of the century, I have been gathering recipes for goodies. Goodies are good, and my mother, sister, husband, and I have a great deal of practice making them.

With all the hullabaloo about fat, carbs, and calories on the rise today, it may seem contrary to write a cookbook filled with buttery cookies and chocolaty cakes. But I do not mean to be contrary. Instead, I fear that all the traditional recipes made for holidays, kids birthdays, potlucks, and whatnot will soon disappear from lack of interest or intolerant suppression.

One of the main reasons I have gathered my goodies into this cookbook is to pass on the recipes that my family members have used for their celebrations through many decades of the 20th century. I am passing them directly to the next generation so they can delight their children and their children's children with these old comfort sweets. These oldies but goodies include home-made hard fudge, mayonnaise cake, pecan tarts, and prize-winning blueberry pie. This is a part of my culture that I don't want to loose in the frenzy for "thin." My own philosophy about "thin" is that it is highly overrated. Recent studies are now showing that those who are slightly overweight live longest. And I would add, live happiest.

Several of my family members participated in a certain subculture of the late 20th century—the hippie subculture of the 1960s and 1970s. Today's health food revolution began with the hippies, back-to-the-landers, communards, and organic farmers of that period. The organic food movement has not only survived, it has now become part of mainstream culture, thus Whole Foods, Trader Joes, and other major chains that sell organic only foods.

Some of the early hippie recipes were experiments, and I have included one in this book—Purist Hippie Carrot Cake. Yes, it is not the tastiest cake in the book, but at the same time, it took some ingenuity to concoct a reasonable cake that contained no eggs, sugar, butter, or oil. Using the natural sweetness of dates, raisins, and organic applesauce, these hippie cake makers discovered some reasonably good alternatives to sugar.

Hippie mothers, including me and some of my sisters, were dead set on cutting the sugar in the kids diets. I have to say, we were pretty successful. Maybe too successful. My son and at least one of my nieces have absolutely no taste for cake, cookies, or other goodies…um…except for certain Christmas cookies and …oh yeah, those pies. The point being that goodies are not for every single day, they are for special occasions, and celebrations, and any other excuse you can think of.

The real simple reason I started working on this cookbook was because I gave my Kitchen Aid mixer to my son, Christopher, and his girl, Emily. They are now fully responsible for making the Christmas cookies. But as I reviewed my dog-eared, batter-splattered recipe cards with all the chicken-scratched handwriting, I decided it was time to commit these treasures to digital format. And then so many of the recipes were from my sisters and mother, I decided to include recipes from all my six sisters, my mother, my gourmet-cook husband, and some very close friends who contributed to my son's childhood.

So here they are, my humble offerings. Indulge, delight, and good night!

Specialty Drinks

✦

Lemonade for a Crowd

Fresh lemonade is a must for summer picnics and barbecues, and you usually need lots. This satisfying drink is always best when made with fresh, just-squeezed lemons. You don't need an expensive juicer for squeezing the lemons, although a juicer can save you time. Just invest in an inexpensive hand juicer, or get a man with large muscular hands to do the work.

Lemonade can often take on more meaning than just it's refreshing, sweet-tart taste. It signals summer. It always reminds me of those hot Midwestern summers when my nine brothers and sisters and I ran free from sunup to sundown with the other fifty or so kids on the block. We roamed the streets and alleys of Chicago's far southwest side and played so intensely we often forgot to go to the bathroom until it was too late. Then, sometimes, in the late afternoon when we started to loose steam and just lay down under the big elm tree in the front yard watching those giant Midwestern cumulous clouds change shape, Mom would bring out a pitcher of fresh-squeezed lemonade for the whole crowd. This is that recipe. Drink it and weep!

- 10 lemons, washed under warm water and halved
- 1 ½ gallons water
- 2 cups sugar
- 1/3 cup honey
- 1 teaspoon vanilla
- Thin lemon slices for garnish

Combine water, sugar, honey, and vanilla in a non-reactive saucepan (stainless, not aluminum), and bring to a simmer over medium heat. Cook, stirring occasionally until the sugar and honey are dissolved, about 10 minutes. Remove from heat, cover, and let steep for 30 minutes to 1 hour.

Squeeze the juice from each lemon half into the steeped mixture and discard rinds. Strain the lemonade into a pitcher so all seeds are removed. Chill for at least 1 hour. The lemonade will keep for several days.

Serve in ice-chilled glasses garnished with lemon slices. Makes 1½ gallons.

Uncle Dick's Thick-As-Thieves Egg Nog

Here is another drink that creates memories and sometimes just blots them out. Beware, this stuff can be potent. With all the frothy foam this recipe whips up, your guests, may not realize how much actual liquor they're drinking, so go easy. Guaranteed to get everyone in the Christmas spirit fast!

- 3 Tablespoons sugar
- 4 egg yolks
- ½ cup bourbon
- ½ cup cognac
- ½ cup rum
- ½ pint heavy cream
- 4 egg whites

Mix sugar, egg yolks, and liquor together and refrigerate for 30 minutes. While waiting, whip the ½ pint of heavy cream to soft peaks. Whip egg whites to soft peaks. Fold refrigerated mixture into whipped cream. Fold in egg whites. Sprinkle each cup with nutmeg and allspice. Makes 10 plus cups.

Cousin Courtney's Killer Rum Martini: Before Sunrise

Inspired by Uncle Dick's potent egg nog, cousin Courtney came up with this original martini. It's one of those drinks that goes down really easily but can have you passed out on the kitchen floor in no time (despite rumors, this has never happened to cousin Courtney). Courtney's fantasy when sipping Before Sunrise is that she is sitting (or maybe not just sitting) on the beach in the Cayman islands next to Bruce Willis watching the sunrise. You can make up your own fantasy, and this drink is guaranteed to speed you on your way to fantasyland.

- 1 ounce of Bacardi rum
- 1 ½ ounce of Malibu rum
- The juice of 1 fresh-squeezed lime or 1ounce of Rose's lime juice
- 1 ½ ounce of cranberry juice

Shaker Version
Fill cocktail shaker with ice. Add all ingredients. Shake vigorously until the cocktail shaker is cold on the outside. Pour through shaker strainer, leaving the ice in the shaker.

Mixing Version
Refrigerate all ingredients beforehand. At cocktail time, add all ingredients into an elegant glass pitcher. Stir well with glass rod.

Breakfast Treats

✦

Uncle Dick's Lakeside Waffles

Every Sunday morning in Lakeside, Michigan, my family and our guests gathered at the little half-circle breakfast table, brilliantly designed to assure maximum communication with the cook, and waited for that first waffle made from scratch by Uncle Dick. As simple as these waffles appear to be, it is not just the ingredients that count. The technique and the instruments also figure in the success of each waffle. So, if you have a good waffle iron, make these. If you don't have a waffle iron, get a high-quality one, and you'll make the perfect waffle every time. Except the first one, of course.

- 1 cup white flour
- 1 ¾ teaspoons baking powder
- 2 eggs
- 1 cup milk
- 3 Tablespoons corn oil
- Pinch of salt

Plug in waffle iron. Mix all ingredients together leaving the batter somewhat lumpy. When the waffle iron is hot, spoon on batter to cover 2/3 of the center of the iron. Close iron and wait till waffle iron indicates it is ready. Remove waffle by gently lifting with fork. The first waffle is often not perfect, but it is lucky. The person who eats the first waffle has always been known to have the most wonderful day.

Aunt Rose's Hippie Cinnamon Crunchy Granola

I have very fond memories of visiting my sister Rose at her central Wisconsin commune, Karma Farm, back in the day. These pure-food pioneers had a large organic garden where they grew sunflowers for their seeds. The farm had its own beehives that produced organic honey. These folks toasted their own wheat germ bought at the hippie-run health food store in Madison, Wisconsin. None of these ingredients were available in any "straight" grocery store back then. Now, nearly forty years later, you can run right out and get all of these ingredients already toasted and ready, at any Whole Foods or Trader Joes.

Let us give thanks and credit to these early efforts of my own family members and their friends to create the alternative society which is now part of the mainstream. If you have only eaten store-bought, boxed granola, you haven't really tasted the goodness of fresh granola made with love and care with all organic ingredients. Thank you aunt Rose.

- 4 cups uncooked rolled oats
- 1 cup grated coconut
- 2 cups walnuts or pecans, broken or coarsely chopped
- ½ cup raw, hulled sesame seeds
- 1 cup raw, hulled sunflower seeds
- 1 teaspoon salt
- ¾ to 1 cup canola oil
- ¾ cup honey to taste
- 2 teaspoons cinnamon
- ¼ to ½ cup toasted wheat germ (optional)
- ¼ cup flax seeds for fiber (optional)

Prepare

Preheat oven to 350 degrees and spray two heavy-duty cookie sheets with cooking oil. Or use a paper towel dipped in oil and rub a very light coat of oil over the cookie sheets.

Mix Granola

In a large mixing bowl, mix all dry ingredients together and add the canola oil. Mix thoroughly, then add the honey. The honey/oil mixture is what makes the granola more or less crunchy, so you can experiment with this. You want real crunchy. The mixture will be thick, and you can knead it with your hands if necessary to thoroughly combine.

Bake Granola

Using a big spoon or spatula, spread the mixture as thinly as possible on the two cookie sheets. Bake at 350 degrees for 30 minutes.

Before you start baking, remind yourself that the worst outcome of this recipe is burning the whole batch. Burnt granola is one very big disappointment. To prevent this, be prepared to monitor the baking process by checking the granola every 5 or 10 minutes. Lift a layer on each cookie sheet and look at the color on the bottom. If one batch is turning golden brown after only 10 or 20 minutes, turn down the temperature slightly and switch the two cookie sheets from top to bottom and back to front. Usually one batch will be cooking nicely and the other is burning. So be aware.

Half way through cooking, turn all the granola over with a spatula. Continue to monitor till the granola is done. It is done when it is golden brown all over. The mixture should be crisp and very crunchy. Remove from oven, and immediately turn over granola several times in the pan as it cools, separating clumps as you go. After thoroughly cooling, put in sealed container to keep fresh. Stays fresh for 3 to 4 weeks. But don't worry about it getting stale, it won't be around too long.

Authentic Hippie Whole Wheat Bread

Put away the bread machine and get into making bread the way the pioneers (and the hippies) did. This recipe takes a good portion of the day, so you'll need to decide beforehand to put aside a day for baking bread. You can do other things in between risings, but give the dough the full time it needs to rise.

Making bread is not only a great opportunity for parent-child interaction (i.e. quality time), but it also qualifies as a major cultural learning experience. After kneading and watching bread rise, your kids will understand how much work goes in to making one of the most important foods in every single human culture around the globe. Knowing how to make bread is a major human survival skill.

Marie Antoinette may have said "Let them eat cake," when told the people had no bread. She missed the mark so obtusely because she did not understand that bread in all its forms – pita, bun, roll, baguette, loaf – is the staff of life without which human nutritional needs cannot be met. So really enjoy your bread baking day. The kids will especially love kneading and punching down the bread. And so will you.

Good luck. And keep trying. If it doesn't turn out well the first time, try again. Bread making takes practice, and there is always another day. If it turns out well, slice a piece for yourself and slather the warm bread with Tupelo honey. This is the taste of what it was like to be a back-to-the-land hippie woman surviving out in the country circa 1969.

Helpful Hints

Tip 1: Go out just before you start the bread and buy very fresh yeast. Old dead yeast can ruin the bread as well as your whole day.

Tip 2: To scald milk, heat in pan slowly just till it starts to bubble. Do not let boil.

Tip 3: You'll need a large counter or an extra-large bread board to knead the bread on. This is your kneading board.

Ingredients
- ½ cup butter
- ½ cup brown sugar
- ¼ cup honey
- 1 Tablespoon salt
- 2 cups scalded milk
- 4 cups stone ground whole wheat flour
- 2 pkgs. dry yeast
- 2-3 cups unbleached flour

Before you begin, offer your first born to the all bountiful bread goddess to assure success. You are going to need it.

Combine butter, brown sugar, honey, salt, scalded milk, and 2 cups of the whole wheat flour in your Kitchen Aid electric mixer. Use the bread attachment – the hook. If you don't have a Kitchen Aid mixer, you can use your electric mixer, but it might break. This is a heavy-duty dough. If you are really in shape, hand mix the dough until it is thoroughly combined. If not, get two or three people to take turns mixing. Neither the pioneers nor the hippies had Kitchen Aid mixers, so for the real authentic experience, do this manually. If you were not in shape, you will be.

Let mixture cool to lukewarm before adding the yeast. Too much heat will kill the yeast. Add yeast and beat again until smooth and creamy. Cover bowl with warm damp towel. Place bowl in warm corner and let rise for 30 minutes. The dough should be about double its original size when fully risen. It may rise over the bowl top. This is good. Punch dough down. Punching down means exactly what it says. Make a fist and punch it right into the middle of the puffed up dough till all the air comes out.

In a separate bowl, mix together the remaining 2 cups of whole wheat flour with the unbleached flour and add enough of the flour mixture to the dough to make the dough stiff enough to handle on the board. Turn out the dough onto your kneading board and knead in as much of the remaining flour as you can. Kneading is the key to bread making. It consists of two things. First, pushing and pulling the dough, folding it over on itself, and generally beating it up so as to develop the gluten. Second, getting all the rest of the flour into the dough. Do this for a good five minutes.

Grease a big bowl with butter and place the dough in the bowl. Turn the dough in the bowl to grease the top. Cover again with a damp towel and let rise until doubled, probably 30 minutes. Punch down well. Turn greased side up and let rise again until light. Turn dough out on board and knead lightly. This might be a good time to preheat the oven to 325 degrees.

Divide dough into two balls and let rest for about 10 minutes. Form into loaves. Place in two greased loaf pans. Let rise again in pans until almost double. Don't punch down. Bake 15 minutes at 325 degrees, then turn oven up to 350 degrees and bake for 45 minutes. Remove from pans and let cool. Makes two large loaves.

Susan's Bran Muffins

Susan Borland is the ultimate new Renaissance women. When she was a girl, she went out and caught fish for her family's supper. Later she became a musician and played Blues and Rock in the country and in the city. But Susan's greatest talent among many is her gourmet touch. She has her own professional kitchen, and her pastries are legendary. I warn you, these bran muffins are kick-ass. No more constipation for anyone.

If you cannot find the All Bran and Bran Buds cereals, you might be able to get bulk bran and bran buds in your Whole Foods or Trader Joe's. Although the recipe does taste better when you use Crisco, Crisco has gotten a bad rep for being unhealthy. So if you are concerned, go to your local health food store and ask for a shortening that is healthier. I found a good one.

This is a big-batch recipe that can be stored in the refrigerator for up to two weeks. This way you can be sure to keep all your family regular by cooking a small batch of muffins each morning. Susan's aunt used to do this and with great success. So make this big batch and keep your family happily regular.

- 1 cup Crisco (or butter)
- 3 cups sugar
- 2 cups All Bran cereal
- 4 cups Bran Buds cereal
- 5 cups flour
- 5 teaspoons baking soda
- 4 cups (one quart) buttermilk
- 2 cup boiling water
- 4 eggs
- 3 teaspoons salt

Preheat oven to 350 degrees. Boil one cup of water. In a very large bowl, mix all ingredients together. Use cupcake papers or grease each cup of a cupcake pan. Or, buy the aluminum foil cupcake papers that stand on a cookie sheet and can be substituted for a cupcake pan. Spoon batter into each cup and fill to top of paper. Bake at 350 degrees for 15 to 20 minutes. Store batter in refrigerator for up to two weeks, and use a little every morning for instant muffins. Eat for breakfast, lunch, and dinner. The absolute cure for constipation and the way to stay regular. Makes about 3 dozen.

Blueberry Poppy Seed Brunch Cake

I've included a couple of blueberry recipes in this book for good reason. Blueberries are said to be anti-cancer food, and I try to eat as many as I can, in season and out. We usually buy a flat of blueberries in Michigan in July and freeze them. Come January, my husband Dick (also known as Uncle Dick) gets up early on Sunday morning and warms the house as well as our tummies with this treat.

Freezing fresh blueberries, by the way, is so simple and quick. After washing, sorting, and removing all stems, just spread blueberries onto a cookie sheet and set into the freezer. Do the same with the next cookie sheet and stack it on top of the first. Next morning, pack the frozen blueberries in separate clear freezer bags. Use the small sandwich bags for when you want to just add them to pancakes. Use the larger freezer bags filled with 4 cups of blueberries for when you want to make a pie or this cake.

Cake
- 2/3 cup sugar
- 1 cup butter
- 2 teaspoons grated lemon peel
- 1 egg
- 1 ½ cup all-purpose unbleached flour
- 2 Tablespoons poppy seeds
- ½ teaspoon baking soda
- ¼ teaspoon salt
- ½ cup sour cream

Filling
- 2 cups fresh blueberries (or frozen, thawed, and drained)
- 1/3 cup sugar
- 2 teaspoons flour
- ¼ teaspoon nutmeg

Glaze
- 1/3 cup powdered sugar
- 1 to 2 teaspoons milk

Prepare

Preheat oven to 350 degrees. Grease and flour bottom and sides of a 9- or 10-inch springform pan. A springform pan is one with high sides that has a gizmo on the side that locks the pan closed. Make sure the pan is locked when you pour in the dough.

Make Cake

In your Kitchen Aid mixer bowl or a large bowl, beat sugar and butter until light and fluffy. Add lemon peel and egg. Beat 2 minutes at medium speed in the Kitchen Aid or on high with a hand mixer.

In a separate medium bowl, combine 1½ cups flour, poppy seeds, baking soda, and salt. Add to butter mixture alternately with sour cream. Spread batter over bottom and 1 inch up sides of greased and floured springform pan, making sure batter on sides is ¼-inch thick.

Make Filling

In medium bowl, combine all filling ingredients. Spoon over batter.

Bake Cake

Bake at 350 degrees for 40 to 55 minutes until crust is golden brown. Cool slightly. Remove sides of springform pan.

Make Glaze

In small bowl, combine powdered sugar and enough milk so that the glaze is of desired drizzling consistency. Blend until smooth. Drizzle over top of warm cake. Serve warm or cool. Serves 8.

Aunt Patti's Blueberry Coffee Cake

My younger sister, Patti, and her family celebrate blueberry season once a year with this luscious treat. But first they spend a weekend in July picking Michigan blueberries. Of late, however, as the "kids" are all grown up, I hear they just buy a ten-pound flat of already picked blueberries. That's cricket with me. They're still good, fresh Michigan berries.

Cake Ingredients
- ½ cup butter
- 1 cup sugar
- 2 eggs
- 1 cup sour cream
- 2 cups flour
- ½ teaspoon salt
- 1½ teaspoons baking powder
- ½ teaspoon baking soda
- 1 teaspoon vanilla
- 1 can blueberry pie filling
- 2 cups (1 pint) fresh blueberries

Topping Ingredients
- ¼ cup butter
- ½ cup sugar
- 1 teaspoon cinnamon
- ½ cup flour
- ½ cup chopped pecans

Make Cake
Preheat oven to 350 degrees. In your Kitchen Aid or a large bowl, cream together butter, sugar, eggs, and sour cream. Set aside. In a separate bowl, mix together flour, salt, baking powder, and baking soda. Blend flour mixture into butter-sugar mixture. Add vanilla. Spread 2/3 of cake mix into a medium rectangular baking pan.

In a third bowl, mix together the can of blueberry pie filling and the 2 cups of fresh blueberries. Spread blueberry mixture on top of cake mix in a layer. Spread the remaining 1/3 of the cake mixture on top of the blueberries.

Make Topping and Bake

Combine all the topping ingredients. Spread over the cake mixture layer. Bake at 350 degrees for 40 to 50 minutes.

Aunt Kathleen's Maryknoll Breakfast Bread

My oldest sister, Kathleen, was a Maryknoll nun for a short time, and when she left the convent, she brought home with her one of the simplest, most delicious breakfast bread recipes ever. I don't know if it's the buttermilk, the brown-sugar topping, or some special grace bestowed by the nuns, but this quick bread is always a hit.

- 2½ cups flour
- ¾ cup sugar
- ½ cup brown sugar
- ½ teaspoon salt
- ½ teaspoon nutmeg
- ¾ cup vegetable oil
- 2 eggs
- 1 teaspoon baking soda
- 1 teaspoon baking powder
- 1 cup buttermilk

Preheat oven to 350 degrees. Grease and flour two 8-inch round or square pans.

Make the Topping

In a large bowl, mix the flour, sugar, brown sugar, salt, and nutmeg. Add the vegetable oil gradually, mixing until crumbly. In a separate bowl, set aside ¾ cup of this mixture for the topping.

Make the Bread

In the large bowl containing the remaining mixture, add the eggs, baking soda, baking powder, and buttermilk. Mix until smooth. For variety, you may want to mix fresh or thawed frozen blueberries into the bread mixture before pouring into the pans. Pour into two greased and floured pans. With a fork, drizzle the ¾ cup of topping over the mixture. Add finely chopped nuts if you like.

Bake the Bread

Bake at 350 degrees for about 25 minutes or until a toothpick stuck in the middle comes out clean.

Banana Nut French Toast with Peanut Butter

This recipe was inspired by a sunny, perky little restaurant that opened up right in my South Loop neighborhood recently. This place is so popular for brunch that I can hardly get out of my building on Saturdays and Sundays because of the crowd waiting for tables.

Talk about comfort food, this is the ultimate. Use this recipe whenever your Banana Nut Cake (included here in the Cakes section) is going stale and your bananas have gone to mash. Make this for breakfast, lunch, or dinner. It's chock full of good healthy potassium-rich bananas and protein-filled peanut butter. Probably lots of calories, but even small amounts are very filling and delicious.

- 8 Banana Nut Cake slices (See Cakes) or any nut bread slices
- 3 eggs, lightly beaten
- 3 or 4 very ripe bananas
- 2 cups pancake syrup
- 1 cup peanut butter

Beat the eggs with a fork in a wide-mouthed bowl. Cut 1-inch slices from a leftover banana nut cake loaf or use whatever bread or quick bread you have around. Put the peanut butter in a small shallow serving dish. Slice the bananas and, if they are not real mushy, put them in the microwave for 50 seconds to make them mushy.

With a fork, dip each cake or bread slice into the beaten eggs making sure the slice is just covered front and back. Do not leave the cake to soak in the eggs. Just make sure the slice is lightly covered in egg. Quickly transfer each slice to a heated skillet. Cook each side of the slice until golden brown, about a half a minute. If not serving immediately, remove slices from skillet, pile them on a plate, and put them in the oven to keep warm.

When ready to serve, dish two slices of toasted cake or bread out on each dish. Cover each slice with the mushy bananas. Heat the syrup in the microwave just before serving and pour over slices. Put the peanut butter on the table for those who want the full protein rush. Serves 4.

Christmas Cookies

✦

Aunt Alice's Almond Crescents

This is the cornerstone of a great Christmas cookie repertoire. If you can follow all the steps, and make sure the cookies are thoroughly whitened with plenty of powdered sugar absorbed into them, you can be confident that you will have the best cookie in any contest or cookie exchange. These are good cookies to start in October or November so you'll have them for Christmas. The recipe makes five dozen or more.

This cookie is not just about mixing ingredients, it takes skill. And even with all the tips I'm providing here, it may take a couple of baking sessions to really master the techniques. Anyone can become a great cookie maker with practice.

Important Notice: Don't ever give this recipe out to anyone outside your family. Give them the Hazelnut Almond Crescent recipe included here if they ask, and they will never know the difference. But your cookie will always be better.

Tip 1: You must have all the proper cookie-making equipment. This includes:
- A marble rolling pin that is placed in the freezer at least 30 minutes before the cookie dough is rolled. These rolling pins are readily available at your nearest kitchen store.
- An old-fashioned glass rolling pin with room inside for ice cubes is acceptable, but try to find one of those.
- A large (20-in. x 20-in. minimum) rolling surface, preferably a cold marble slab
- A cool kitchen
- A sturdy metal pastry lifter
- A Kitchen Aid mixer, or a strong arm and a pastry blender
- A cookie spatula (optional, but saves on burned fingers and broken cookies)
- Lots of Christmassy cookie tins

Tip 2: Follow all the instructions meticulously especially:
- How long the dough is refrigerated (at least 2 hours).

- How to roll up the jellyroll. This takes practice.
- How to form the crescents without too much handling.
- How to handle the cookies when sugaring them so they don't all break and you don't burn your fingers.

Tip 3: Always use **100% butter**. Christmas is no time for margarine. Your reputation will be ruined if you substitute margarine for butter.

Tip 4: You may want to make the cookies over a two-day period. The first day, make the dough and put it in the refrigerator covered with a thin kitchen towel. On day two, roll the dough and sugar the cookies. Otherwise plan on using a whole day to make these cookies and get the kids to help.

Ingredients
- 1 cup butter
- 2/3 cup sugar
- 2 eggs
- 4 teaspoons almond extract
- ½ teaspoon salt
- ¼ teaspoon of nutmeg
- 1 cup chopped almonds
- 2 cups flour
- A whole lot of powdered sugar for covering 5 dozen cookies

Prepare
Put the rolling pin in the freezer and chop the nuts if necessary. Store-bought chopped nuts may be too big for these delicate cookies, so if they are large pieces, chop them a bit more. Grease two to four cookie sheets and set aside. Determine where you will roll dough or get out marble slab if you have one.

Mix Dough
Cream the butter and sugar in the Kitchen Aide or a large mixing bowl. Add eggs, salt, almond extract, and nutmeg. Mix well. Add nuts. Add all the flour and mix well.

Chill Dough and Preheat Oven
Divide the dough into two dough balls and return to the same bowl. Cover bowl with saran wrap or a damp dishtowel and refrigerate for at least two hours or overnight. After taking dough out of refrigerator, preheat the oven to 350 degrees. Let the dough warm to room temperature for flexibility.

Roll Dough

Spread plenty of flour on the rolling surface, and remove the rolling pin from the freezer. Rub the rolling pin all over with plenty of flour. Roll out each dough ball into a long rectangular shape about 1/8-inch thick and about 12 inches long by 6 inches wide. Use your pastry lifter to make sure the bottom of the dough does not stick to the board. Keep pushing flour under the dough with the pastry lifter.

Create the Jelly Roll

Now you are going to roll up the dough into a long, many-layered jelly roll. Start at one end of the rectangle and roll up the dough. Use the pastry lifter as you roll to prevent the dough from sticking to the surface. Push flour under the roll to prevent sticking. This takes years of practice so don't cry when it all breaks up on you. If it breaks, it is too dry or too warm. Either add a little water, or put the dough back into the refrigerator until it gets cold.

Cut and Shape Crescents

With a sharp knife, cut off ½-inch slices from the jellyroll. Roll each small slice with just the tips of your fingers on the flat of your other hand. The key is not to handle the dough too much. But you also must make sure each crescent stays together. So you may have to press weak spots together. The crescents should be fat in the middle and thin at both ends.

Place crescents on the greased cookie sheets. Use two cookie sheets. Place one on the top rack of the oven and one on the bottom rack. While they are cooking, you can grease and fill the other two cookie sheets so they can go right in as soon as the first batch is done. If you only have two sheets, that's OK too.

Bake the Cookies

Total cook time for each batch should be 12 minutes. Set the oven timer for 5 to 6 minutes so you can switch the cookie sheets at the halfway mark. When the buzzer rings, switch the sheets from the top to the bottom rack and back to front. Set the timer again for 5 or 6 minutes. The cookies will be somewhat white when they are done, and they should be firm. They will continue to get firmer as they cool.

Sugar the Cookies

You will need to get help with this sugaring step as the cookies need to be sugared when hot. Since this recipe makes a lot of cookies, you'll also need to be preparing more crescents to go into the oven while sugaring the cookies coming out. Really, get help.

While the first batch of cookies is cooking, set up three large plates. Fill the first and second plate with mounds of powdered sugar and leave the third plate empty. As soon as the cookies come out of the oven, use your cookie spatula to place 5 or 6 cookies onto the first plate. Using the tips of your fingers roll each cookie around to completely coat it with sugar. The sugar will soak in quite a bit. Transfer the cookies to the second plate and let them cool a bit while you sugar cookies on the first plate.

Roll all the cookies through the first two sugarings. The second sugaring should produce a white, sugar-covered crescent with not much melting sugar. Place the sugared cookies on the empty plate and allow to cool completely. If a cookie turns dark and you can see that the sugar has soaked in, put it back into the second sugar plate and roll it until it is fully white with sugar.

After the cookies have cooled on the plate, put them in your Christmassy tins or plastic storage containers. You can store them in the freezer for up to 3 months. Store them separately from other cookies because the powdered sugar gets all over any other cookies.

Now, take a rest and swear that you will never make these cookies again. But you will next year because everyone will beg you to make your special Christmas crescents again and again.

Hazelnut Almond Crescents

Adapted from "Hazelnut Almond Crescents" featured in Fine Cooking—Holiday, *Tauton Press, Newton, CT, Winter 2006.*

If you are in a hurry and need quick and easy almond crescents to give away as presents in a tin, these will suffice. Also, you can pair these with the Almond Sables recipe which uses the same basic dough with different kinds of sugars and without the nuts. The basic dough recipe below is three batches worth. So you can make two batches of Hazelnut Almond Crescents and one batch of Almond Sables. Or you can triple the recipe where indicated below and make three batches of these easy almond crescents. Each batch makes 24 to 28 cookies.

Basic Almond Dough (Makes 3 batches)
- ½ cup granulated sugar
- ½ teaspoon salt
- ¾ cup whole almonds
- 1½ cups (3 sticks) unsalted butter, cut in large chunks and slightly softened
- 4 teaspoons vanilla
- ¼ teaspoon almond extract
- 3 cups bleached all-purpose flour

Hazelnut Almond Crescents Only
Use one third of the basic almond dough plus the ingredients below for one batch. If making all three batches as almond crescents, triple the ingredients below.

- 1 cup toasted hazelnuts, chopped medium coarsely
- A lot of confectioners' sugar

Make the Basic Dough
Combine the sugar and salt together and process in a food processor for about 30 to 60 seconds until it looks powdery. Add the whole almonds and process for about 20 seconds until they are finely chopped. Transfer this

processed mixture to the Kitchen Aide or large mixing bowl. Using the dough paddle (white flat, heart-shaped), add the butter, vanilla, and almond extract. Mix until butter is smooth, scraping the bowl if necessary.

Add the flour and mix until a soft dough begins to form around the paddle. Divide the dough into thirds, each one about 1¼ cups. Take one third of the dough and follow the directions below for one batch of Crescents. Freeze the rest of the dough until you want to make Almond Sables or more Crescents. If you want to make all three batches of Crescents now, use all the dough and triple the recipe from here on out.

Form the Crescents

Using your hands, add the hazelnuts to the mixture working the nuts into the dough. Shape tablespoons of dough into fat crescents and put them in a container lined with waxed paper. Crescents should be fat in the middle and taper off at each end. You can get this shape by rolling a ball of dough in the palms of your hands. When you place the dough onto the waxed paper bend it into a big C. Cover and refrigerate for at least two hours or overnight.

Bake the Crescents

When you are ready to bake, take the crescents out of the refrigerator and arrange on an ungreased cookie sheet. Position two racks in the oven, and preheat the oven to 325 degrees. Let the crescents warm to room temperature while the oven is heating.

Total cooking time is 20 to 22 minutes. To assure even cooking, set your timer to the halfway mark in baking time—10-11 minutes. When the buzzer rings, rotate the cookie sheets switching the top sheet with the bottom and turning each sheet from front to back. Don't forget to set the timer again for 10 to 11 minutes for the second half of the cooking time.

Bake the cookies at 325 degrees for 20 to 22 minutes total until the tops are lightly colored and the bottoms are golden brown. Let the cookies cool on the cookie sheet for about 5 minutes after baking, then roll the cookies in the confectioners' sugar. You may find that the confectioners' sugar melts into the cookies. When this happens, roll again in more powdered sugar.

Almond Sables

Adapted from "Almond Sables" Fine Cooking—Holiday, *Tauton Press, Newton, CT, Winter 2006.*

The Basic Almond Dough recipe below is three batches worth and is the same dough you use for the Hazelnut Almond Crescents. If you are making a lot of Christmas cookies, pair these with your Almond Crescents and you get three batches of two different cookies from one dough mixing. If you want to make all three batches of Almond Sables, you'll need to triple the recipe where indicated below. Each batch makes 24 cookies.

Basic Almond Dough (Makes 3 batches)
- ½ cup granulated sugar
- ½ teaspoon salt
- ¾ cup whole almonds
- 1½ cups (3 sticks) unsalted butter, cut in large chunks and slightly softened
- 4 teaspoons vanilla
- ¼ teaspoon almond extract
- 3 cups bleached all-purpose flour

Almond Sables Only
Use one third of the basic almond dough and the ingredients below, for one batch. If making all three batches of Almond Sables, triple the ingredients below.

- 1 ½ Tablespoons granulated sugar
- ¼ cup turbinado sugar or any large-grained sugar

Make the Basic Dough
Process the sugar and salt in a food processor for 30 to 60 seconds until it looks powdery and a little finer. Add the almonds and process for about 20 seconds until they are finely chopped. Transfer this processed mixture to the Kitchen Aide or large mixing bowl. Using the dough paddle (white flat,

heart-shaped), add the butter, vanilla, and almond extract. Mix until butter is smooth, scraping the bowl if necessary.

Add the flour and mix until a soft dough begins to form around the paddle. Divide the dough into thirds, each one about 1¼ cups. Take one third of the dough and follow the directions below for one batch of Sables. If you are making all three batches of Almond Sables, use all the dough and triple the recipe from here on out.

Make the Sables

Use the back of a large spoon or a rubber spatula to mash the 1½ tablespoons of granulated sugar into the dough until it's evenly dispersed. On a lightly floured surface, shape the dough into a log about 6 inches long and 1¾ inches in diameter. Wrap the log in waxed paper or foil. Refrigerate for at least two hours or overnight.

Remove the cookies from the refrigerator. Put the ¼ cup of turbinado sugar on a flat surface such as a tray or clean countertop. Turbinado sugar is just any large grained sugar that makes for a better presentation on Christmas cookies. Roll the dough log in the sugar, pressing it in so it adheres to the outside edges only.

Cut the log into ¼-inch slices and arrange the slices at least 1 inch apart on an ungreased cookie sheet. Do not get any sugar on the top or bottom of the cookies and brush sugar off the cookie sheet. Excess sugar will burn very quickly in the oven. Preheat the oven to 350 degrees. Let the cookies sit at room temperature until the oven heats.

Bake the Sables

Bake the cookies at 350 degrees for 12 to 15 minutes total until the edges are golden brown. To assure even cooking, set your timer to the halfway mark in baking time, so 6 to 7 minutes. When the buzzer rings, rotate the cookies sheets switching the top sheet with the bottom and turning each sheet from front to back. Don't forget to set the timer again for 6 to 7 minutes for the second half of the cooking time.

Let the cookies sit on the baking sheet for a minute or two before transferring them to a cooling rack with your cookie spatula. Let cool completely before storing.

Cinnamon Mini Palmiers

Adapted from Fine Cooking—Holidays, *Tauton Press, Newton, CT, Winter 2006*

These delicate, cinnamon-sugared delights are always a hit. They're relatively easy, and the only real caution is, don't burn them. They should be a deep golden brown color after baking. Each cookie can bake at a different rate, so watch them like a hawk while baking.

This cream cheese dough recipe makes three batches worth, with each batch making 24 cookies. So 72 cookies in all. This recipe requires two 2-hour chilling times, so plan accordingly. Making the dough one day and baking the next would be especially advantageous for this cookie.

Cream Cheese Dough
- 3 ¾ cup bleached flour
- 3 Tablespoons granulated sugar
- 3/8 teaspoon salt
- 1½ cups (3 sticks) cold, unsalted butter
- 12 oz. (1½ bricks) Philadelphia cream cheese (use bricks not tubs)
- 1½ cups granulated sugar
- 3 pinches of salt

Combine the 3 tablespoons of sugar, flour, and salt in your Kitchen Aid or large mixing bowl. Using the paddle attachment (white enamel flat paddle), mix briefly to distribute the ingredients. Cut each stick of butter into eight pieces and add to bowl. Mix on low speed for about 3 minutes until most of the mixture resembles very coarse bread crumbs with a few larger pieces of butter the size of hazelnuts. Cut the cream cheese into 1-inch cubes and add to bowl. Mix on medium-low speed for about 30 to 60 seconds until a shaggy-looking dough begins to clump around the paddle.

Dump the dough onto the work surface, scraping the bowl. Knead a few times to incorporate any loose pieces. There should be large streaks of cream cheese. Shape the dough into a fat cylinder, 6 inches long and about 3½ inches in diameter. Portion the dough into three equal rolls by cutting the cylinder into three equal parts. Wrap each roll in waxed paper and refrigerate for about 2 hours. Each roll should be cold and slightly firm but not rock hard.

Remove the dough from the refrigerator and square off each separate roll by pressing the round edge on the counter four times. If necessary, let the dough sit at room temperature until pliable enough to roll. Transfer one tablespoon of the sugar to a small cup and mix in the salt. Set aside.

Do the following with each roll:

Fold the Palmiers

Sprinkle the work surface liberally with some of the remaining sugar. Set the dough on the sugared surface and sprinkle it with more of the sugar. Now, roll the dough into a 24" x 8" rectangle that is less than 1/8-inch thick. Turn the dough frequently. Resugar both the dough and the work surface liberally. Use the sugar generously to prevent sticking and to ensure that the cookies will caramelize properly in the oven. Trim the edges of the rectangle evenly.

Mark the center of the dough with a small indentation. Starting at one short edge, fold about 2½ inches of the dough almost one-third of the distance to the center mark. Without stretching or pulling, loosely fold the dough over two more times, leaving a scant ¼-inch space at the center mark. Likewise, fold the other end of the dough towards the center three times, leaving a tiny space at the center. The dough should now resemble a long, narrow open book. Fold one side of the dough over the other side, as if closing the book. You should have an 8-layer strip of dough about 2½ inches wide and 8 inches long.

Sprinkle the remaining sugar under and on top of the dough. Roll gently from one end of the dough to the other to compress the layers and lengthen the strip to about 9 inches. Wrap the dough loosely in waxed paper (not plastic wrap, which might cause moisture to form on the outside of the dough and dissolve the sugar). Refrigerate the dough for two hours.

Bake the Palmiers

Position racks in the upper and lower thirds of the oven and heat the oven to 375 degrees. Remove the dough from the refrigerator, unwrap it, and use a sharp knife to trim the ends evenly. Cut 1/3-inch slices like this:

- Mark the dough at 1-inch intervals
- Cut three slices from each inch

On two ungreased or foil-lined cookie sheets, arrange the slices 1½ inches apart. Bake or 8 to 10 minutes until the undersides are golden brown.

Rotate the cookies sheets from top rack to bottom and front to back halfway through baking.

Remove the pans from the oven and turn the cookies over. Sprinkle each one with a pinch or two of reserved salt-sugar mixture. Return the sheets to the oven until the cookies are a deep golden brown, another 3 to 5 minutes.

During this baking, watch the cookies very carefully. Be sure to rotate the pans and watch for any signs of burning. If the cookies brown at different rates, remove the dark ones and let the lighter ones continue to bake. Transfer the cookies to a rack and let cool completely. Store airtight.

Aunt Alice's Particularly Good Pecan Tarts

This cookie is easy to mix, but it takes quite a bit of time to press the tart dough into the tartlet pans. This is the second-most favorite Christmas cookie for my family after Aunt Alice's Almond Crescents. As such, it is a must to have these around on Christmas Eve and Christmas Day in the my household.

One thing you'll find is that the dough and the filling do not always come out even. You may have more filling than dough. But that's OK. You can either make more dough or toss the extra filling. Don't get into the habit of eating the sugary filling that's left over. You will probably get sick.

This is a good one to get the kids involved in because it takes a lot of thumb-work to get the tart dough flattened into those mini tart pans. Which reminds me. You will need two additional cookie-making instruments for this recipe:

Special Utensils
- Two to four mini tart pans
- One or two tart tampers (optional) or very strong thumbs

Crust
- 2 cups flour
- 1 large, 8-ounce Philadelphia cream cheese brick (do not use tubs)

Filling
- 1 cup brown sugar
- 1 cup butter
- ¼ teaspoon vanilla
- 1 cup pecan pieces, chopped fine

Make the Crust
Mix the flour and cream cheese together until dough is crumbly but shapes up when you pinch it together. Put about 1 teaspoon of dough into each tart cup in the tart pans. Using the tart tamper or your thumbs, shape

the dough over the bottom and up the sides of each tart cup. Use enough dough to leave a little edge on each tart. Shape the edge like a pie crust edge.

Preheat the oven to 350 degrees only after all the crust is pressed.

Make the Filling

Soften the butter and mix in the brown sugar and vanilla. Chop the pecan pieces so that they are relatively small. You want a lot of nut pieces in each tart. At the same time, you don't want the nut pieces to be too small. Mix the pecan pieces into the butter-sugar mixture. Do not substitute other nuts. These are strictly pecan tarts. Makes about 2 ½ dozen cookies.

Assemble the Tarts

Scoop about 1 teaspoon of the pecan filling into each tart. Fill the cup about ¾ full. If you fill it too full it will bubble out all over the place when cooking. It will probably do this anyway, but less is more in this case.

Bake the Tarts

Bake the tarts for 20 minutes at 350 degrees until brown around the edges. If you overfilled the tarts or for whatever reason the pecan filling boils all over the tart pan, remove from the oven after they are fully cooked and just gently spoon the goo back into the cups. All will be well.

And, whatever you do, do not cool these on an open windowsill. That knave will surely be around to steal these tarts.

Swedish S Cookies

These are cookie-press cookies, so you'll need a good cookie press. You can find cookie presses in cook-store catalogues, for very reasonable sums. You want a sturdy, light, metal or plastic press with lots of good nozzles and very good instructions with pictures. This is a good starter recipe for cookie-press cookies because you only need to use the one star nozzle. The dough comes out in long strings, and you can form it into all kinds of shapes. You should probably practice the first time you try pressing. Just put any messed up dough back in the press and do over. I usually make letters for the kids first initials and hope they don't break. Breakage is a liability of these cookies, so you want to make your Ss fairy large and substantial.

Note: The S in these cookies probably stands for Sweden, but we have always interpreted the S as meaning Stevens. My son, whose family name is the Scottish Skeens, has always insisted it stands for Skeens. If you are not Swedish or a Stevens or a Skeens, you can interpret this S as Secret, Scrumptious, or Swell. Whatever, we are all S's together here.

Additional Utensils
- A sturdy, well-made cookie press

Cookie Dough
- 1 cup (2 sticks) cool butter
- ½ cup sugar
- 1 egg, well beaten
- 2½ cups flour
- ¼ teaspoon salt
- 1 cup semi-sweet chocolate chips
- ½ cup toasted, ground pecans

Preheat the over to 375 degrees. Cream together the butter and sugar. Add the egg, flour, and salt. Stir well to combine. Stuff dough into cookie press. Using your cookie press with the star nozzle, press dough onto an ungreased cookie sheet in an S pattern about 2 1/2 inches long. Place cookies about an inch apart. Bake for 10 minute until the edges are barely golden brown. Transfer to a rack to cool.

In a double broiler melt the chocolate chips and set out a bowl full of the toasted ground pecans. Dip one end of each cookie into the hot chocolate and then into the ground pecans. Return to rack or plate to dry. Cookies can be frozen in an airtight container, with waxed paper between each layer for up to 6 months. Defrost 30 minutes before serving. Makes 64 cookies.

Spritz Cookie-Press Cookies

This is the traditional dough for putting in a cookie press. You can also use the Swedish S cookie dough which is very similar. For Christmas, I always use the tree and wreath discs. The Sawa cookie press is a good brand with a sturdy, metal tube. I usually bunch the dough into a long log just slightly smaller than the tube of the cookie press. Then all you have to do is place it into the tube.

When pressing the cookies, set the press to the double notch setting. Sit the press down on the cookie sheet with the feet firmly in place then pull the trigger until it stops. Lift the press firmly and do the next one. The first cookie is always a mess, but after the second one, just move along consistently pressing once for each cookie. Get into a rhythm. Remove mistakes from the sheet and add back into the dough.

Special Equipment
- Sawa or other sturdy cookie press
- Cookie spatula

Dough
- 2 ¼ cups all-purpose flour
- ¾ cups sugar
- ¼ teaspoon baking powder
- ½ teaspoon salt
- 1 cup butter
- 1 egg
- 1 teaspoon vanilla

Mix together flour, sugar, baking powder, and salt. Blend in butter until mixture resembles coarse crumbs. Break the egg into a measuring cup. If it does not measure ¼ cup, add water up to the ¼ line. Stir the egg into the crumb mixture and add the vanilla. Beat well. Chill the dough in refrigerator at least one hour.

Remove dough from refrigerator and let it warm a bit until it becomes pliable. For tube cookie presses, you can roll the dough into a long round shape slightly smaller than the circumference of the cookie press tube. The dough should be pliable, but if at any time it becomes too soft, re-refrigerate.

Push the dough through the press onto an ungreased cookie sheet using the various shapes that come with the cookie press . Bake at 350 degrees for 10 to 12 minutes. Makes 5 dozen cookies.

Chocolate Nut Sugar Crisps

This recipe is easy compared to some Christmas cookie recipes, but the cookies have the same delicious taste as more complicated concoctions. These also have a nice dark chocolate color that adds variety to your array of Christmas goodies.

- 2 ½ cups flour
- 3 Tablespoons unsweetened cocoa
- 1½ teaspoons baking powder
- ½ teaspoon salt
- 1 cup butter, softened
- 1 ½ cups sugar
- 1 large egg
- 4 squares (4 oz.) semi-sweet chocolate
- ½ cup sliced, chopped almonds

Preheat oven to 375 degrees. Grease two cookie sheets. Combine flour, cocoa, baking powder, and salt in a bowl. Set aside. Use your Kitchen Aid or hand mixer to beat butter and sugar until light and fluffy. Beat in egg. Stir in flour mixture.

Divide dough in half and freeze for 10 minutes. Shape dough into two 9-inch logs. Wrap in wax paper or foil, and freeze for about 1 hour until firm. Remove from refrigerator and cut log into slices. Arrange slices on greased cookie sheets and bake at 375 degrees for 8 to 9 minutes until edges are set.

Melt chocolate in a small microwave bowl about 1 to 2 minutes on high. Stir until smooth. Spread hot chocolate on tops of cookies, covering them with a thick layer of chocolate. While the chocolate is still hot, sprinkle the nuts around the outside edges of the cookie leaving the center nut-free.

Swedish Nut Balls

What can I say? These are fast, easy, and delicious. They also add variety to your Christmas cookie array because they are round rather than flat. People pop them into their mouths like popcorn and inhale the powdered sugar till they choke, so make them small, and have plenty of egg nog around to make them go down smoothly.

- 1 cup (2 sticks) cold, lightly salted butter, cut into chunks
- 1 ¾ cups powdered sugar
- 2 cups flour
- 1 teaspoon vanilla
- 1 cup ground pecans

Preheat the oven to 325 degrees. In a bowl, cream together butter and ¾ cup of the powdered sugar. Add the flour, vanilla, and ground pecans. Stir to combine.

Shape dough into balls, using a slightly rounded teaspoon for each. Place 2 inches apart on an ungreased cookie sheet. Bake until the edges turn gold, about 20 minutes.

Transfer cookies to a rack to cool. Cookies can be frozen in an airtight container, with wax paper between the layers for up to 6 months. If you do this, defrost for 30 minutes before serving.

Just before serving cookies, place the remaining cup of powdered sugar in a plastic bag. Add several cookies and shake gently to dust with sugar. Repeat with all the cookies. Makes about 5 ½ dozen.

Really Good Rugelach

This is a fun recipe and takes about 30 minutes of prep time, but you have to add in the 1 hour to chill the dough. The kids will like helping to roll each cookie, and it is easy enough for them to do, even if a bit sloppy. But isn't that part of the fun? Baking time is about 20 minutes. Makes about 4 dozen.

- 2 ½ cups flour
- 1 cup (2 sticks) cold butter, cut up
- 1 pkg. Philadelphia cream cheese (8 oz. brick)
- 1 Tablespoon sugar, plus sugar to roll on
- ¾ teaspoon cinnamon
- 9 Tablespoons seedless raspberry preserves
- 1 cup finely chopped pecans

Process flour and butter in Kitchen Aid or large bowl until mixture resembles coarse meal. Add cream cheese and process until dough holds together. Divide dough into thirds. Flatten into three disks. Wrap in foil or saran wrap and refrigerate for 1 hour.

Preheat over to 350 degrees. Grease two large cookie sheets. Combine 1 Tablespoon sugar and cinnamon in cup. Set aside. Sprinkle a clean towel or a large counter generously with regular granulated sugar. Roll each disk into a 10-inch circle. Spread 3 tablespoons of raspberry preserves evenly on top of each disk. Sprinkle with 1/3 cup pecans and 1 teaspoon of the cinnamon sugar mixture.

Cut each disk into 16 wedges. Roll up each wedge from the outer wide edge to the point. Transfer to cookie sheet. Bake 15 to 20 minutes until golden brown. Cool. Makes 48 cookies.

Egg Nog Logs

This is a real Christmassy Christmas cookie. It's fun and kind of messy to decorate. But you'll be proud of the beautiful results. These really taste like egg nog (rum and all). So have patience. It takes about an hour plus chill time. Make the frosting during chill time. Then have a real good time decorating. If you can find green jimmies and some of those tiny red balls for decorating, all the better. But, if not, they still look good with just the frosting and some nutmeg. Baking time is 15 minutes. Makes 5 dozen.

Dough
- 1 cup butter, soft
- ¾ cup granulated sugar
- 1 Tablespoon dark rum
- 1 teaspoon vanilla
- 1 teaspoon nutmeg
- 1 large egg
- 3 cups flour

Frosting
- ¼ cup butter, soft
- 2 ½ cups confectioners' sugar
- 1 teaspoon dark rum
- 2 Tablespoons milk
- 1 teaspoon vanilla

Decorations
- Small red balls
- Green jimmies
- Nutmeg

Make Cookies
Preheat oven to 350 degrees. Beat butter and sugar in Kitchen Aid or large mixing bowl until light and fluffy. Beat in rum, nutmeg, vanilla, and egg. Stir in flour. Divide dough into six pieces. Wrap in foil or saran wrap, and refrigerate for 30 minutes.

On lightly floured surface, shape each of the six pieces of dough into a rope ½ inch in diameter. Cut 3-inch logs from each rope. Arrange 2 inches apart on ungreased cookie sheet. Bake 13 to 15 minutes until light brown. Cool.

Make Frosting

Beat the butter and 2 cups confectioners' sugar together. Add the rum and vanilla and beat until smooth. Add milk and beat in remaining confectioners' sugar until spreadable

Decorate Cookies

Spread frosting on each cooled cookie. Run fork down the length of cookie to simulate bark. Sprinkle with nutmeg. At one end of each cookie, add one red ball and two or three green jimmies to make a holly sprig.

Christmas Cookie-Cutter Cookies

These are fun and easy. The recipe produces very thin, crisp, treats that are good anytime. Kids will especially like this recipe because they can cut the cookies into all kinds of shapes and sizes. Let them plan which shapes they'll use, cut the cookies, and sprinkle the topping on. Use Christmas-themed cookie cutters and green and red sparkle sugar instead of cinnamon for Christmas.

Equipment
- Wax paper or saran wrap
- Aluminum foil
- Pastry cloth
- Cookie cutters large and small

Dough
- 1¾ cup flour
- 2 teaspoons baking powder
- ½ teaspoon salt
- 1 stick unsalted butter
- Rinds of 2 lemons, grated
- 1 Tablespoon lemon juice
- 1 cup granulated sugar
- 1 large egg
- 2 Tablespoons whipping cream

Cinnamon-Sugar Topping
- 1 Tablespoon granulated sugar
- 1/3 teaspoon cinnamon
- Pinch of nutmeg

Christmas Cookie Decorations
- 1 egg white
- Water
- Red sparkle sprinkles
- Green sparkle sprinkles
- Chocolate jimmies

Grate rinds of two lemons. Set aside. Mix flour, baking powder, and salt in a bowl and set aside. In the Kitchen Aid, beat butter, lemon rind, and lemon juice together. Add sugar. Beat in egg and whipping cream. Add the flour mixture and mix well. Gather the dough together and wrap it in wax paper or saran wrap and refrigerate overnight (or for at least 2 hours).

Preheat oven to 375 degrees. Line cookie sheets with aluminum foil shiny side up. Roll dough on pastry cloth or other surface to 1/8-inch thick. Use your large cookie cutters, placing them all on the dough first before the final cutting to assure efficient use of dough. Do not re-roll dough. Use smaller cookie cutters to cut cookies from any leftover dough between the large cutouts.

For Cinnamon-Sugar Topping

Prepare the cinnamon-sugar topping by mixing all the ingredients together. Sprinkle over tops of cookies. Bake the cookies at 375 degrees for 10 to 13 minutes. Store in airtight container.

For Christmas Cookies Toppings

For Christmas cookies, use red and green sparkle sugars and chocolate jimmies instead of cinnamon. Sprinkle these on only after baking. Mix egg white and water to make a sticky, gelatinous paste. After cookies cool thoroughly, brush each with paste just before applying sparkles and jimmies.

Rachel's Chocolate Candy Cane Cookies

Peppermint butter cream is sandwiched between homemade chocolate cookies. Then the sandwiches are rolled in crushed candy canes. Delicious and delightful.

Cookie Ingredients
- 1 ¾ cups all purpose flour
- ½ cup unsweetened cocoa powder (preferably Dutch-process)
- ¼ teaspoon salt
- 1 cup sugar
- ¾ cup (1½ sticks) unsalted butter, room temperature
- 1 large egg

Filling Ingredients
- 1 cup plus 2 tablespoons powdered sugar
- ¾ cup (1½ sticks) unsalted butter, room temperature
- ¾ teaspoon peppermint extract
- 2 drops (or more) red food coloring
- ½ cup crushed red- and white-striped candy canes or hard peppermint candies

Prepare
Preheat oven to 350 degrees. Line two baking sheets with parchment paper.

Make Cookies
Whisk flour, cocoa, and salt in medium bowl to blend. Using your Kitchen Aid or a large mixing bowl and an electric mixer, beat sugar and butter until well blended. Beat in egg. Add dry ingredients and beat until blended. Refrigerate dough for one hour.

Remove from refrigerator and let warm. Scoop out dough by level tablespoonfuls, then roll into smooth balls. Place balls on prepared baking sheets, spacing about two inches apart. Using bottom of glass or hands, flatten each ball into 2-inch rounds (edges will crack). Bake until cookies no longer look wet and small indentation appears when tops of cookies are lightly touched with fingers, about 11 minutes. Do not over bake or cookies will become too crisp. Cool on sheet for 5 minutes. Transfer chocolate cookies to racks to cool completely.

Make Filling

Using your Kitchen Aid or a large mixing bowl and an electric mixer, beat powdered sugar and butter until well blended. Add peppermint extract and two drops of food coloring. Beat until light pink and well blended, adding more food coloring by dropfuls if darker pink color is desired. Spread two generous teaspoons of filling evenly over flat side of one cookie to edges; top with another cookie, flat side down, pressing gently to adhere. Repeat with remaining cookies and peppermint filling. Place crushed candy canes on plate. Roll edges of cookie sandwiches in crushed candies. Candies will adhere to filling. Makes about 18 sandwich cookies.

Everyday Cookies

✦

Mrs. Fields Two Hundred Fifty Dollar Cookies

This recipe was the talk of the town in the early 1990s because of the story of the lady who was taken unawares. The lady in question got her revenge and that is why you now have this recipe. Here is the story that appeared on the early Internet.

> A friend inquired about obtaining the recipe below and was told by a sales clerk at Mrs. Fields that the recipe was available for $25. The clerk gave her the phone number to call to order her recipe. The friend called the number and was told that the recipe was, indeed, available to the public. The friend gave her credit card number and purchased the recipe.
>
> The recipe arrived and so did the credit card receipt indicating that she had paid $250 rather than $25. When she protested to Mrs. Fields, they were unresponsive. After contacting her attorney, she was told the deal was legal and she would have to pay the price. Her revenge is that she is giving this recipe to everyone she possibly can.

With the Internet just becoming available to the general public at that time, she was able to distribute the recipe widely. So, for you and your descendents, the recipe is free. But I seriously suspect that the recipe here is not really the complete Mrs. Fields recipe. But whatever, they are delicious.

This is a very large batch—industrial sized. It makes 112 medium-sized cookies, and you definitely need a Kitchen Aid mixer to mix all the flour and oatmeal it requires. Because it makes so many, I have used these as filler when sending big tins of Christmas cookies.

- 2 cups butter
- 2 cups sugar
- 2 cups brown sugar

- 4 eggs
- 2 teaspoons vanilla
- 4 cups flour
- 5 cups oatmeal, ground to powder
- 1 teaspoon salt
- 2 teaspoons baking powder (a pinch more to make softer)
- 2 teaspoons baking soda
- 24 oz. bag of chocolate chips
- 1 plain Hershey bar (8 oz.), grated
- 3 cups chopped nuts (walnuts are good)

Prepare

Preheat oven to 350 degrees. Pulverize the oatmeal into powder using a food process or blender. Do this in small batches. You may have to empty each batch into a bowl while grating the next small amount. Grate the Hershey bar using the large holes on a stand up grater. Do this fast before the chocolate melts in your hands.

Make Dough

In the Kitchen Aid, cream together the butter, sugar, and brown sugar. Add the 4 eggs and the vanilla. In a separate bowl, thoroughly combine the flour, powdered oatmeal, salt, baking powder, and baking soda. Add this mixture to the wet ingredients in the Kitchen Aid and beat well. This may take some time to mix, and it will fill the bowl to the top. Do not get discouraged. If your Kitchen Aid sounds stressed, clear the batter from the beater, scrape down the sides with a spatula, and keep going. Your Kitchen Aid was made for this kind of heavy duty recipe.

Add the chocolate chips, grated Hershey bar, and nuts, and continue to beat until all is incorporated.

Place golf-ball sized dough balls 2 inches apart on ungreased cookie sheets. These are rather large cookies, but if you want to make smaller cookies, make smaller balls. Bake at 350 degrees for 6 to 8 minutes. Makes 112 cookies.

Toll House Cookies with White Chocolate Chips

Adapted from the back of the Nestles Chocolate Chips bag.

These are probably the most popular home-made cookies in the United States and probably in the world. This recipe is very close to the one on the back of the Nestles chocolate chips bag, but I have added an essential ingredient. And let me stress that this is an essential recipe for every mom to have around to lighten things up when stress is getting you down.

This is a nice, small batch recipe that you can make quickly with ingredients you usually have at hand. Makes about 50 small 2-inch cookies. Many people like to eat these cookies soft right out of the oven and they are great that way. Just make sure you (or your kids) don't burn your tongue on the still-melting chocolate chips. Also, these cookies cool to a nice crisp texture so you can have them both soft out of the oven and crunchy when cool.

- 1 cup plus 2 Tablespoons flour
- ½ teaspoon baking soda
- ½ teaspoon salt
- ½ cup softened butter
- 6 Tablespoons granulated sugar
- 6 Tablespoons brown sugar, packed
- ½ teaspoon vanilla
- 1 egg
- ½ cup semi-sweet chocolate chips (Nestles OK, Ghirardelli fabulous)
- ½ cup white chocolate chips (same as above)
- ½ cup chopped nuts (walnuts or pecans)

Preheat oven to 375 degrees. In a small bowl, combine the flour, baking soda, and salt. Set aside. In the Kitchen Aid or large mixing bowl, combine the butter, granulated sugar, brown sugar, and vanilla. Beat until creamy. Beat in the egg.

Add the flour mixture to the Kitchen Aid bowl and mix well. Stir in the chocolate chips and nuts. Drop rounded teaspoonful onto ungreased cookie sheets. Bake at 375 degrees for 8 to 10 minutes. Cool.

Potbelly's Chocolate Chip Oatmeal Cookies

Someone named Laurie Andrews gave me this one. I don't remember who she is or who she is related to. But Potbelly's cookies are good. This is another big batch that makes big cookies. Or, you can make smaller balls and get more cookies. You can also halve this recipe if it looks like it is too cumbersome and too much for your tiny family. Talk about industrial sized -- eight sticks of butter! Nine eggs! 12 cups of oats! Are we feeding the horses? Whew!

- 2 lbs. butter (8 sticks)
- 4 cups sugar
- 2 boxes of brown sugar (16 oz. each)
- 3 teaspoons vanilla
- 9 eggs
- 6 ½ cups flour
- 2 teaspoons salt
- 4 teaspoons baking soda
- 12 cups oats
- 3 ½ cups semi-sweet chocolate chips

Preheat oven to 350 degrees. Mix the first five ingredients together in Kitchen Aid or very large mixing bowl. In a separate large bowl combine flour, salt, and baking soda. Add this dry mixture to the Kitchen Aid bowl. Add the oats a little at a time and mix again. Add the chocolate chips. Place large 2-inch in diameter balls of dough 2 inches apart on ungreased cookie sheets. Flatten each cookie with a spatula. Bake at 350 degrees for 6 to 8 minutes. Don't know exactly how many cookies this makes, but probably a gazillion.

Aunt Patti's Chocolate Chip Coconut Cookies

This recipe contains pecans or coconut or both. It is quick and easy, and you can make the cookies big or small. These are a nice variation on the standard chocolate chip cookies.

- 1 cup butter
- 1 cup sugar
- 1 cup firmly packed brown sugar
- 2 eggs
- ¼ cup milk
- 1 teaspoon maple syrup
- 2 cups flour
- 1 teaspoon baking soda
- 1 teaspoon salt
- 2 cups uncooked quick oats
- 1 cup semi-sweet chocolate chips
- ½ cup pecans (optional)
- ½ cup coconut (optional)

Preheat oven to 375 degrees. In the Kitchen Aid or in a large bowl, beat together butter, sugar, and brown sugar. Add eggs, milk, and maple syrup. Beat until well blended. In another bowl, blend flour, baking soda, and salt. Slowly add dry ingredients to wet ingredients, and beat until well blended. Stir in oats and chocolate chips. You can add the pecans and/or the coconut at this point.

Drop dough in rounded teaspoonfuls two inches apart onto a non-stick cookie sheet. Bake at 375 degrees for 9 to 12 minutes or until golden brown. Cool for 1 minute on baking sheet before cooling on rack.

Peanut Butter Criss-Cross Cookies

My mother used to bake these regularly in the 1950s. I remember from a very early age being allowed to make the criss-crosses with a dinner fork. These are melt-in-your-mouth good and easy to make with ingredients you probably have around. They cool off to a very crisp texture, and really satisfy those peanut-butter cravings you and your kids may experience from time to time. (Hey, I still do!).

- ½ cup brown sugar
- ½ cup granulated sugar
- ½ cup butter
- 1 egg
- 1 cup creamy peanut butter
- ¼ teaspoon salt
- ½ teaspoon baking soda
- 1½ cups flour
- ½ teaspoon vanilla

Preheat oven to 375 degrees. In a small bowl, mix the brown and granulated sugars. In the Kitchen Aid, cream the butter and add the sugar mixture gradually. Blend until creamy. Beat in the egg, peanut butter, salt, and soda. Add the flour and mix well. Add the vanilla.

Place slightly rounded teaspoonfuls onto ungreased cookie sheets. Smash each ball down with the tines of a fork, first one way then the other in a criss-cross pattern. Bake at 375 degrees for 15 minutes until golden brown. Makes about 60 small cookies.

Peanut Butter Pinwheels

I like these because you get such an amazing effect with the black and white swirls that appear in these cookies. It looks like some gourmet pastry chef made them, and really, the technique is a piece of cake (or cookie).

- ½ cup butter
- 1 cup sugar
- ½ cup creamy peanut butter
- 1 egg at room temperature
- 1 Tablespoon milk
- 1½ cups flour
- ¼ teaspoon salt
- ½ teaspoon baking soda
- 1 cup semi-sweet chocolate chips

Cream butter, sugar, and peanut butter in the Kitchen Aid or large mixing bowl. Beat in egg and milk. In a separate bowl mix flour, salt, and baking soda. Add dry ingredients to creamed mixture.

Form dough with hands into long, flat rectangle. Place dough on floured waxed paper and place waxed paper on top. Roll into a 15" by 8" rectangle. Remove top waxed paper and trim dough edges.

Melt chocolate chips in double boiler. Cool slightly. Spread chocolate over dough to edges with spatula. Roll dough into jellyroll like roll. Wrap in wax paper, seam side down. Refrigerate for 30 minutes.

Preheat oven to 375 degrees. Remove jellyroll from refrigerator and roll with hands on the counter until the jellyroll is rounded off. Cut ¼-inch slices. Place slices 1 inch apart on ungreased cookie sheet. Bake 10 to 12 minutes until light golden brown.

Almond Coffee Rum Cookies

It's always good to have a few cookie-cutter cookie recipes to keep kids busy on a rainy spring or snowy winter day. And you will appreciate the rum after the chaos of kids cooking. Don't eat too many of these before driving. And think of how the kids will go right down to their naps. Was I a terrible mother or what?

- 2/3 cup butter
- 1 cup sugar
- 2 Tablespoons strong coffee
- 1 egg
- 3 Tablespoons flour
- 1 generous Tablespoon rum
- 2 ½ cups + 2 Tablespoons flour
- 2 teaspoons baking powder
- ½ teaspoon salt
- ½ cup chopped almonds

Preheat over to 350 degrees. In the Kitchen Aid or large mixing bowl, cream the butter and sugar. In a separate bowl, add the egg, beat well, then blend in the 3 Tablespoons flour, the coffee, and the rum. Add this mixture to the creamed butter. Beat to make a soft batter.

Add the 2 ½ cups of flour, baking powder, salt, and almonds. If necessary, add the extra 2 Tablespoons of flour to make a stiff dough. Chill covered in refrigerator for 1 hour. After removing from refrigerator, roll the dough to 1/8- inch thickness. Cut with cookie cutters or cut into squares. Bake at 350 degrees for 8 to 10 minutes.

Cappuccinos

You do need to acquire or borrow a jellyroll pan for this recipe. These delicious confections are good to serve with coffee or tea and at adult parties. They are somewhat sophisticated yet easy to bake with ingredients on hand. The only ingredient you may have to go out and purchase is the powdered instant expresso coffee.

Special Equipment
- Jellyroll pan

Dough
- 1 cup unsalted, softened butter (2 sticks)
- 1 cup light brown sugar, packed
- 1 Tablespoon powdered instant expresso coffee
- 1 teaspoon vanilla
- 2 ¼ cups flour
- ½ teaspoon baking powder
- ½ teaspoon salt
- 2 cups (12 oz.) semi-sweet chocolate chips

Glaze
- 1 Tablespoon butter
- ¼ teaspoon cinnamon
- ¾ cup confectioners' sugar
- 2 Tablespoons milk

Preheat over to 350 degrees. Grease a 15 ½" x 10 ½" x 1" jellyroll pan.

Prepare Dough
In the Kitchen Aid or large mixing bowl, cream butter, sugar, expresso, and vanilla until fluffy. Add flour, baking powder, and salt and mix well. Stir in chocolate chips. Press dough into the bottom of the greased jelly roll pan. Bake at 350 degrees for 25 minutes until golden brown. Set aside to cool and prepare the glaze.

Make Glaze

Melt butter with cinnamon in a saucepan over low heat. Remove from heat and add alternately the sugar and milk until the glaze is thin and spreadable.

Glaze and Cut

Brush glaze over top of the cooled cappuccinos. Before the glaze sets, cut the sheet into 2-inch bars. When cool, cover pan with foil to store.

Lemon Almond Snowballs

These cookies are decorative and can look like professionally made bakery confections. They are really lemony and combine some of my favorites—lemon, almonds, and chocolate. This is a combination everyone will like. You'll need a pastry bag or a makeshift pastry bag made, very simply, from a plastic sandwich bag with a small hole cut in one of the bottom corner.

Dough
- 1 cup softened butter
- ¾ cup confectioners' sugar
- 1½ cups flour
- ½ cup cornstarch
- ¼ teaspoon salt
- 2 teaspoons grated lemon peel
- 1 cup toasted, blanched almonds finely chopped

Frosting
- 1 cup confectioners' sugar
- 1 Tablespoon lemon juice
- 2 Tablespoons melted butter

Make Dough
Preheat oven to 350 degrees and grease two cookie sheets. In the Kitchen Aid or large mixing bowl, beat butter and confectioners' sugar together until light and fluffy. Add flour, cornstarch, and salt and mix well. Add lemon peel. Shape dough into 1-inch balls. Roll each ball in the chopped almonds. Place cookies 2 inches apart on the cookie sheets. Bake at 350 degrees for 14 to 15 minutes until golden brown. Cool.

Make Frosting
In a bowl, whisk confectioners' sugar, melted butter, and lemon juice until smooth. Spoon into plastic bag and snip end or use a pastry bag. Pipe the frosting across cookies in a continuous zigzag pattern or any other pattern you like. Makes 4 dozen.

Traditional Scotch Shortbread

Shortbread is so easy to make and has a rich, distinctive taste that may appeal more to adults than children. If you are having a tea or afternoon party, these are just the thing. But they are just as good anytime as a snack. You'll really appreciate having a cookie lifter for this recipe.

- 2 cups flour
- ½ cup powdered sugar
- ¼ teaspoon salt
- 1 cup cool butter cut into chunks

Preheat over to 300 degrees. Mix together flour, sugar, and salt. Add the butter, and use your hands or a pastry cutter to combine until the mixture is crumbly. Work into a ball and knead briefly. Pat dough into a ¼-inch flat sheet on an ungreased cookie sheet. Cut into 2-inch squares.

Bake at 300 degrees for 45 minutes. Remove from the over. Immediately re-cut the cookies as they were originally cut. Separate carefully and set on a rack to cool. This is where your cookie lifter comes in especially handy and prevents burned fingers. Cookies can be frozen in an airtight container with wax paper between each layer for up to 6 months. Defrost 30 minutes before serving. Makes about 28 cookies.

Brownies, Rolls, and Bars

✦

Classic Lemon Squares

Lemon squares are about the only thing that can satisfy if you cannot or don't want to eat chocolate. They are a great summer treat and look cheerful. When I was a young mother, I would always envy those women who brought really lovely lemon squares to the potlucks, coffee klatches, and picnics that are inevitable (and sometimes endless) when you have kids. And I always ate about fifty percent of all the lemon squares available. Try to restrain yourself, or you will never get the lemon squares to the party.

Equipment
- Pastry blender
- 9" x 13" baking pan

Crust
- 1½ stick butter, room temperature
- ½ cup powdered sugar
- 1½ cup flour

Filling
- 3 eggs
- 1 ½ cups granulated sugar
- 3 Tablespoons flour
- 1/3 cup lemon juice or the juice of one lemon
- Powdered sugar as needed

Make Crust
Preheat oven to 350 degrees. Mix the butter, powdered sugar, and flour with a pastry blender and pat into 9" x 13" pan. Bake for 20 minutes at 350 degrees. Leave oven on at 350 degrees after removing crust.

Make Filling
Mix eggs, granulated sugar, and flour until thoroughly blended. Add lemon juice and mix well. Pour mixture over baked crust and bake again for 20 minutes at 350 degrees.

Finish

Remove from oven and sprinkle the powdered sugar over top. Cool and cut into squares.

Grandma Alice's Hard Fudge

When all is said and done, I think that all my brothers and sisters would agree that making hard fudge was the most dramatic and rewarding cooking experiences witnessed in our tiny south-side Chicago kitchen.

We all admired Mom's expertise at whipping around from stove to sink, stirring the chocolate with her big upper arms flapping like bird wings. The way she was able to stir the boiling mixture while at the same time throwing in the butter and vanilla was magical. She did all this with about five little kids underfoot all begging to be the first to lick the pan.

Until the very end, we never really knew whether a batch would come out right or if we would get a gloppy mess that was inedible. When Mom made it, we had about a ninety-nine percent chance of success. And when it came out right, there was nothing like it. The smell alone while it was boiling was like no other, and this was the best pan licking you would ever get. Waiting till the actual fudge squares cooled was excruciating unless you had the honor of licking the pan. As number five child, I usually only got to lick the spoon (Woe is me!). When we finally got to dig our teeth into that hard gritty home-made chocolate, it was to die for.

When I grew older and encountered "fudge" in cutesy Victorian-themed shops in upscale tourist towns across the Midwest, I was shocked that anybody could actually sell that soft-assed gloppy substance at a premium price and call it fudge. So in this I can feel superior to all those rich people who are eating glop when I know what fudge really can be. Yes, now I am a fudge snob and always will be. I have the memory of hard fudge home-made in Mom's tiny, linoleum-floored kitchen with the little porcelain-sink and the stove whose pilot light was always going out. (Somehow we all survived.) We may not have been well-off in many ways, but we knew what real fudge smelled like, and we had tasted a little bit of heaven.

As you have probably guessed from the story above, this recipe takes real skill and perfect timing. It is really a candy-making recipe, so you may need to practice before you disappoint the kids with a gloppy mess. There are variations to this, but the bare-bones, tried-and-true version is below.

- 2/3 cup cocoa powder
- 3 cups granulated sugar
- 1½ cups milk
- ¼ stick of butter
- 1 teaspoon vanilla

Prepare the Kitchen

Fill the kitchen sink with cold water, and butter an 8"x 8" pan. Place the 8" x 8" baking pan beside the sink so it is ready when you need it. Measure out the butter and vanilla and put them next to the pan at the sink. Have a clear glass measuring cup or a low bowl of cold water handy next to the stove where you will be boiling the candy.

Boil the Candy

In a 3- or 4-quart saucepan, combine the cocoa powder, granulated sugar, and milk. Bring to a boil and keep at medium boil for about 6 or 7 minutes while stirring constantly.

Test the Candy

While continuing to stir the boiling mixture, test by dropping one or two drips of the candy into a clear glass measuring cup of cold water. With your fingers and thumb, try to make a ball. Test it every now and then, and when you are able to make a firm ball in the cold water, remove from heat and transfer pan to sink full of cold water. Don't forget to turn off the burner.

Stir and Pour Candy

The bottom portion of the pan where the candy is should be fully submerged in the cold water. Be careful not to get any water into the pan. You'll be holding the pan at an angle in the water with one hand and stirring vigorously with the other hand. At some point you'll need a third hand to throw in the butter and vanilla. An assistant would be helpful for this. Or, if you're really fast like my mother was, just stop stirring very briefly and throw in the butter and vanilla.

You will notice that the chocolate mixture has a shine on it when you first start stirring. Keep an eye on this and as soon as the mixture looses its shine and begins to have a flat brown look, pour it quickly into the 8"x 8" pan. The mixture should very quickly crystallize. If it doesn't, throw it back into the pan and stir it in a bit more. Cool thoroughly and cut into small, candy-sized squares.

Lick the Pan

The candy will also crystallize in the sauce pan and on the spoons, so make sure any helpers get a chance to scrape and lick the cooking implements while the candy squares are cooling. This is the only way to distract children from burning their fingers trying to get to the candy while it is cooling. Also, if there are a number of children present, you may have to arbitrate fights over who gets to lick the pan first.

Uncle Dick's Damn Good Brownies

My husband, a.k.a. uncle Dick, was the best cook I'd ever known when I married him. He also was pretty persnickety about everything being "home made." In fact, on the night we met, I had brought a home-made blueberry pie to dinner and everyone praised it highly. Except Dick. He offered to drive me home that night, and on the way he mentioned that the pie was OK except for that dry, store-bought crust. I remember my face reddening with shame in the dark car. Somehow he and I both got over that, and now we are a damn good pie-making dynamic duo. (See Dick's Best Pastry Dough in the Pies and Tarts section.) But I really fell in love with him and his cooking when he fed me his very special damn good brownies. When asked what the secret to his brownies was he replied, "cooking them for exactly 22 minutes, no more, no less." I don't know, every oven is different, but he swears by this timing thing.

Everyone in the my family swears these are the best brownies ever. When our boys went away to college, this was what they missed most. So once in a while Dick would make a batch and send them off in care packages to the various colleges. These are so moist, you almost think it's a mousse pretending to be a brownie. Be sure to follow the directions about lining the pan with aluminum and buttering the aluminum, otherwise you'll never get them out of the pan. If that should happen, just pick up a fork and eat them out of the pan.

- 2 ounces unsweetened chocolate
- 1 stick (½ cup) unsalted butter, plus butter for pan
- 1 cup sugar
- Dash of salt
- ½ teaspoon vanilla
- 2 eggs
- ½ cup flour

Preheat oven to 350 degrees and line an 8"x 8" baking pan with aluminum foil. Butter the aluminum. In a saucepan, melt the chocolate and butter together and cook over low heat while stirring constantly. Remove from heat and thoroughly combine sugar, salt, vanilla, eggs, and flour into the butter mixture. Pour into aluminum-lined pan. Bake at 350 for 22 minutes. Remove from oven and cool. Lift the whole batch out of the pan using the foil. Cut into small squares. This is a lot of concentrated chocolate so, don't overdo. Makes 12 small brownies.

French Chocolate Brownies

Adapted from "Baking: From My Home to Yours" *by Dorie Greenspan, Houghton Mifflin, 2006 and included in* The New York Times Magazine *2006.*

- 1 teaspoon melted butter for brushing pan
- ½ cup flour
- 1/8 teaspoon salt
- 12 Tablespoons butter (1 ½ sticks) cut into pieces
- 6 ounces (6 squares) semi-sweet chocolate, in pieces
- 3 eggs
- 1 cup sugar
- ½ teaspoon vanilla
- 2/3 cup lightly toasted walnuts or hazelnuts (optional)

Place a rack just below the center of the oven and preheat oven to 300 degrees. Line an 8" x 8" baking pan with foil and brush the aluminum with the 1 teaspoon of melted butter.

In a bowl, whisk flour and salt together. Set aside. In top of a double boiler set over barely simmering water, or on low power in a microwave, melt 1½ sticks of butter and chocolate together. Stir often and remove from heat when a few lumps remain. Stir until smooth.

In you Kitchen Aid or large mixing bowl, beat eggs and sugar together until thick and pale yellow. Add chocolate mixture and vanilla and mix at low speed until smooth. Add flour and salt mixture and mix 30 seconds. Finish mixing by hand and add nuts. Pour into prepared pan and bake at 300 degrees for 50 to 60 minutes, until top is dry. Let cool in pan, then lift out and cut into bars. Wrap in foil to store. Makes 12 to 16 brownies.

Aunt Liz's Toffee Bars

Aunt Liz is the baby of my mother and father's brood of ten. When she grew up, she became a pioneer in the nurse-midwife movement which helped to encourage mothers to have their babies in a more relaxed and natural way with less medical intervention. After raising a couple of step children, Liz had her own first baby at age 46. She loves to cook with her frisky young daughter. When they bake these toffee bars together, she says that they make her dance and sing in the kitchen just like our mother used to do. So this recipe is recorded here in my dancing sister's own words as she dictated it to me.

- ½ pound (2 sticks) butter
- 1 cup light brown sugar
- 1 egg yolk
- 2 cups flour
- 1 teaspoon vanilla
- 12 ounces (one bag) semi-sweet chocolate chips
- 1 cup walnuts or pecans, chopped

Preheat oven to 350 degrees. In Kitchen Aid or large mixing bowl, cream together butter and sugar. Add egg yolk, and beat the heck out of the mixture until it looks nice. Sift in flour and mix well while wiggling the hips slightly. Then stir in the vanilla. And now begins the opera singing. (Just pretend your Mom.) Spread batter into 9" x 13" baking dish (Pampered Chef stoneware works great. See Cousin Patience to order Pampered Chef).

Bake at 350 degrees for 25 minutes. Remove pan from oven, and immediately spread chocolate chips evenly over the top of the crust allowing morsels to melt while the cake is still hot. Do not dance or sing during this part or you'll burn something. With a spatula or knife, spread the melted chocolate evenly to the edges. Now sprinkle the nuts over the top. Let cool. And yes, you have to share them. Now you can do a little tap dance!

Chris' Quick and Easy Toffee Bars

Now here is one of the fastest, easiest, short-cut recipes you can get. It is not gourmet, but you don't want gourmet when you have forgotten you are supposed to bring something to that school event or potluck and it's way to late to think of some fancy pants treat. This recipe is exactly right for that situation. It is fast, easy, and they are really good.

- Enough graham crackers to cover bottom of 8" x 8" cake pan
- 1 cup butter
- 1 cup brown sugar
- 1 cup chopped walnuts or pecans
- 6 Hershey bars, broken in pieces

Preheat oven to 350 degrees. Line two 8" x 8" cake pans with graham crackers. Melt butter in saucepan. Add brown sugar and nuts and bring to a boil. Boil for 3 minutes. Pour over graham crackers. Bake at 350 degrees for 9 minutes. Remove from oven and immediately lay Hershey bars over the top of the hot cake letting them melt naturally. Cut into squares before it cools. Makes 18 bars in 20 minutes.

Theresa's Blueberry Boy Bait

My good friend Theresa's family has been making this recipe for at least 100 years (possibly more). And her family has proliferated nicely as she is one of seven. Then she went and had three kids herself. So, you see it works. Here is what Theresa has to say about Blueberry Boy Bait.

> *"I honor all the women in my family for all the thousands of times they have cooked up Blueberry Boy Bait over the past 100 years. And an honorable mention goes to the many happy and mosquito-itchy blueberry picking trips we took with my Uncle Al in central Wisconsin."*

This is just one more of the many blueberry recipes I have included in this book. I've done this for two reasons: first, we live in the Midwest and we all love local, fresh, hand-picked blueberries; and second, blueberries are especially good for your health as they are anti-carcinogenic. And of course there is the third and most important reason I include so many blueberry recipes. Blueberries are delicious whether cooked or just picked.

Without the Midwestern, fresh-picked blueberries, I am not sure the "boy bait" part of the recipe will work as well. Those blueberries are thought to be somewhat magical, and some think they are an aphrodisiac. But, go ahead if you want and use blueberries from Maine or Chile, and see if they don't work just as well.

- 1½ cups sugar
- 2 cups flour
- 1½ sticks butter
- 2 teaspoons baking powder
- 2 eggs
- ¼ teaspoon salt
- 1 cup milk
- 1 teaspoon vanilla
- 2 cups fresh blueberries

In the Kitchen Aid or a large bowl, blend together sugar, flour, and butter with pasty mixer. Set aside ¾ cup of mixture. Blend remainder of mixture with baking powder, eggs, salt, milk, and vanilla. Pour into a 9" x 13" baking pan. Arrange blueberries on top of dough. Sprinkle the ¾ cup of reserved butter mixture on top. Bake at 350 degrees for 30 minutes. Cool. Cut into squares. Feed to boys who you want to marry your daughters.

Cakes

✦

Apple Tube Cake

Don't know where I got this one, but it is always good to have a recipe for a nice lightweight tube cake. The tube pan is also known as an angel food cake pan; it has a tube up the middle and the cake rises high.

I discovered that angel food cakes are really full of hot air and much lighter than most other cakes. This also makes them much less fattening. If you are trying to lose weight but you love your goodies, try this cake without the glaze and see if it doesn't satisfy. Also, angel food cake is great for strawberry short cake. The cake absorbs the strawberry sauce well and looks like a large serving. But it's just all that hot air.

An apple-corer is great to have to save some of the work of peeling and cubing the apples. These instruments are inexpensive and effective. Some old hippies and purists like to leave apples unpeeled, but this is inappropriate when baking this dish.

Batter
- 1½ cups vegetable oil
- 3 eggs
- 2 cups granulated sugar
- 3 cups flour
- 1 teaspoon baking soda
- 1 teaspoon salt
- 2 teaspoons vanilla
- 3 cups peeled, diced apples
- 1 cup black walnuts, finely chopped

Glaze
- 1 cup buttermilk
- ½ cup butter (1 stick)
- 1 cup sugar
- ½ teaspoon vanilla
- ½ teaspoon baking soda

Prepare

Preheat oven to 325 degrees. Peel apples and dice. Chop black walnuts if necessary. Grease and flour a 10-inch tube pan (angel food cake pan).

Make the Batter

In your Kitchen Aid or in a large bowl, combine oil, eggs, and sugar. In a separate bowl, combine sugar, flour, baking soda, and salt. Add the dry ingredients to the oil mixture and mix well. Fold in vanilla, apples, and walnuts. Pour into prepared pan.

Bake Cake

Bake at 325 about 1½ hours or until wooden toothpick inserted in center comes out clean. Cool in pan 30 minutes.

Make Glaze

In a large saucepan combine all glaze ingredients. Heat to boiling and boil for 2 minutes. Cool for 10 minutes and pour over cake. Cake can be cut into 12 or 16 pieces.

Banana Nut Cake

You always need at least one recipe that uses really ripe bananas because bananas notoriously go bad sooner than you want. Whenever I see that the bananas have gone too ripe, I pull out this quick bread recipe. Despite the sugar, bananas are good for you with all that potassium.

You can make this recipe as a cake or put it in loaf pans and make it as a quick bread. Make it as a quick bread when you want to use any left over slices for the *Banana Nut French Toast with Peanut Butter* recipe included here in the Breakfast Treats section.

- 2 ¼ cups flour
- 2 teaspoons baking powder
- ¼ teaspoon baking soda
- ½ teaspoon salt
- ½ cup soft butter (1 stick) at room temperature
- 1 cup sugar
- 2 eggs
- ½ cup chopped nuts
- 1 ¼ teaspoons vanilla
- 2 Tablespoons milk
- 1 cup mashed bananas

Prepare

Preheat oven to 350 degrees. Soften the butter and chop the nuts if necessary. Mash the bananas. Grease and lightly flour two 8" x 8" cake pans or two loaf pans. Use loaf pans if you plan to use leftovers for *Banana Nut French Toast with Peanut Butter* (See Breakfast Treats).

Make Batter

In a medium bowl mix together the flour, baking powder, baking soda, and salt. Set aside.

In the Kitchen Aid or a large mixing bowl, cream the butter and sugar on medium speed for 3 minutes. Add eggs and continue to mix on medium speed for 2 minutes. Scrape sides and bottom of bowl. Add chopped nuts, vanilla, and milk. Mix in ¼ of the dry ingredients. Stir on low speed for 1 minute. Blend in the remaining dry ingredients and bananas alternately on low speed for 4 minutes or until batter is smooth. Pour batter into prepared pans.

Bake Cake

Bake at 350 degrees for 30 minutes or until wooden toothpick comes out clean.

German Sweet Chocolate Cake

This is a specialty cake I always like to make in the winter for my own birthday in February. It is a milk-chocolaty cake with a delicious coconut pecan frosting that I especially like. The proper way to make this cake is to only frost the tops of the cake layers and not the sides. With the less frosting you really can savor the great chocolate taste in the cake itself. And it looks good because it is a big, tall, three-layer cake.

German Chocolate Cake
- 1 package (4 oz.) German sweet chocolate baking chocolate
- ½ cup boiling water
- 2 cups flour
- 1 teaspoon baking soda
- ¼ teaspoon salt
- 1 cup (2 sticks) butter, softened
- 2 cups sugar
- 4 eggs separated
- 1 teaspoon vanilla
- 1 cup buttermilk

Coconut Pecan Frosting
- 1 can (12 ounces) evaporated milk
- 1 ½ cups sugar
- 3/4 cup (1½ sticks) butter
- 4 egg yolks, slightly beaten
- 1½ teaspoons vanilla
- 2 2/3 cups coconut
- 1½ cup chopped pecans

Prepare
Preheat oven to 350 degrees. Line three 9-inch round cake pans with waxed paper. Grease sides of pans.

Melt Chocolate

In a double boiler, combine chocolate and water and melt. Cool. Or, in large microwave bowl, microwave chocolate and water on high for 1½ to 2 minutes or until chocolate is almost melted. Stir after each minute, and stir till chocolate is completely melted after removing from microwave.

Make Cake Batter

In Kitchen Aid or large mixing bowl, cream together butter and sugar on medium speed until fluffy. Add egg yolks, one at a time, beating well after each one. Stir in chocolate mixture and vanilla. In a separate bowl, stir together flour, baking soda, and salt and add alternately with the buttermilk to the chocolate mixture. Beat after each addition until smooth. Beat egg whites with electric mixer until they form stiff peaks. Fold into batter carefully. Pour into three 9-inch round pans.

Bake Cake

Bake at 350 degrees for 30 to 35 minutes. Remove from oven and immediately run spatula between cakes and sides of pans. Cool for 15 minutes.

Make Frosting

In a saucepan, combine milk, sugar, egg yolks, butter, and vanilla. Cook and stir over medium heat until thickened, about 12 minutes. Remove from heat. Add and thoroughly combine the coconut and chopped pecans. Cool until thick enough to spread, beating occasionally. Makes 4½ cups. This is enough to frost just the tops of the three layers of cake.

Frost Three-Layer Cake

After thoroughly cooling, frost the tops of two of the three layers. Place one frosted layer on top of the other. Place the last layer on top of the cake and frost just the top not the sides. Serves 16.

Chocolate Yin-Yang Hippie Cake

This is, for the most part, a standard chocolate cake and I have included a selection of either quick chocolate or quick white frosting. Use both frostings to make a Yin-yang cake.

The Yin-yang sign used in eastern philosophy became popular in the 1960's and 1970's as a sign of peace, tranquility, and wholeness. It represented opposites working together in harmony. The Yin-yang sign is a black swish with a white swish in the opposite upside-down position. The two swishes are totally integrated into each other. The black swish has a white eye and the white swish has a black eye. The Yin yang sign is shown at the end of this recipe.

Chocolate Cake
- 1 cup unsweetened cocoa powder
- 2 cups boiling water
- 1 cup melted butter
- 2 ½ cups sugar
- 4 eggs
- 2 teaspoons vanilla
- 2 1/3 cups flour
- 2 teaspoons baking soda
- ½ teaspoon baking powder
- ½ teaspoon salt

Quick Chocolate Frosting
- Several sweet chocolate bars
- Cream or milk
- 1 teaspoon vanilla

Quick White Frosting
- 2 cups confectioner's sugar
- 3 Tablespoons butter
- 1/4 teaspoon salt
- 2 teaspoons vanilla

Prepare

Preheat oven to 350 degrees. Line two 9-inch round baking pans with buttered wax paper.

Make Cake

Mix cocoa with boiling water, stirring with wire whip until smooth. Cool in refrigerator while preparing other ingredients. In Kitchen Aid or large mixing bowl, beat butter with sugar, eggs, and vanilla on high speed for 5 minutes. In a separate bowl, mix together baking soda, baking powder, and salt.

On low speed, add the dry ingredients alternately with cocoa mixture, starting and ending with flour. Do not over beat. Divide batter into the two baking pans. Bake at 350 degrees for 30 to 35 minutes or until toothpick stuck in middle comes out dry. Cool in pans about 10 minutes. Remove cakes and cool on racks.

You can use these cake layers together by frosting them with any frosting just as you would any cake. Frost one layer, place the other on top, then frost top and side of whole two-layer cake.

Make Quick Chocolate Frosting

In a double boiler, melt chocolate bars until smooth. Add vanilla and mix thoroughly. Cool slightly, then spread on cake. If the chocolate seems too stiff, beat in a little cream or milk before you spread the frosting.

Make Quick White Frosting

Standard quick white icing is the easiest because it does not require cooking. You can use this icing for any cake. In a bowl beat the butter until soft, then add the confectioners' sugar gradually until creamy. If the icing is too thin add more confectioners' sugar. If too thick, add a little cream or milk. When mixture is satisfactory for spreading, add the salt and vanilla. Frost cooled cakes with a spatula or blunt knife. For a glossy appearance, dip your spatula in hot water while you are frosting.

Yin-Yang Frost

When preparing to frost the top layer of this cake, cut a cardboard circle the size of the cake pan and draw the Yin-yang line on the cardboard. Use the picture of the Yin-yang provided here to create this line. Cut the cardboard on the curved line and place one half of the pattern on the cake. With a knife, trace the curve onto the top of the cake to keep the demarcation lines separate. Leave the half-cardboard piece on the cake while you frost one side. Then put the other half of the cardboard pattern on the cake and frost the other side. Here is a nice Yin-yang symbol you can use as a model for making the pattern on cardboard for your frosting.

When you finish frosting, don't forget to put the eyes of the opposite color onto each side of the cake.

Grandma Alice's Marvelous Mayonnaise Cake

Our mother, Alice Roche Allgaier, for whom I was named, made this cake for many a birthday for her ten kids. It's a quick, easy, and delicious cake that has no pretensions to gourmet. That's why it appeals to kids. They don't need super-chocolated mousses or flourless chocolate cakes. Still, this is a rich, dark, moist cake made as a flat sheet cake so it can be cut into many small squares for those larger parties. Be sure to use the good real mayonnaise and don't do "lite" as this would be a desecration of the real, rich flavor you get from real mayonnaise.

- 2¼ cups unsifted flour
- 1 teaspoon baking soda
- ¼ teaspoon baking powder
- 1 2/3 cup of sugar
- 3 eggs
- 1 teaspoon vanilla
- 1 cup of real mayonnaise
- 4 (1 ounce) squares semi-sweet chocolate, melted
- 1 1/3 cup water

Prepare
Grease and flour a 9"x 13" baking pan and preheat oven to 350 degrees.

Make the Cake
In your Kitchen Aid or large bowl, beat sugar, eggs, and vanilla at high speed for 3 minutes or until light and fluffy. In a separate bowl, mix the flour, baking soda, and baking powder and set aside. At low speed, beat in mayonnaise and melted chocolate. Add flour mixture in four additions alternately with water. Pour batter into baking pan.

Bake the Cake
Bake at 350 degrees for 45 minutes. Cool. Frost top with a standard vanilla or chocolate frosting.

Chocolate Sour Cream Bundt Cake

Adapted from Williams-Sonoma Kitchen, Williams-Sonoma, Inc. San Francisco, CA, 2006

I've included this cake because it is always handy to have a fancy Bundt cake recipe that is just full of decadent chocolate, sour cream, and stuff like that. You may someday need to impress a boss, shine at the potluck, or treat a birthday child. This recipe came with the Nordic Ware Anniversary Bundt cake pan I bought just to make this delicious cake. Did you know that Nordic Ware invented the Bundt cake pan in 1966? It is a heavy cast-aluminum pan made after the German Bundform, a mold used to create traditional German desserts. So, I am dedicating this recipe to my father and the German (Austrian) side of my family.

Special Equipment
* A sturdy bundt cake pan

Cake Ingredients
* 1 cup cocoa powder
* 1 cup semi-sweet chocolate, finely chopped
* 1 cup boiling water
* 2¼ cups all-purpose flour
* 1½ teaspoons baking soda
* 1¼ teaspoons kosher salt
* 2½ sticks unsalted butter
* 2½ cups firmly packed light brown sugar
* 5 eggs lightly beaten
* 4 teaspoons vanilla
* 1½ cups sour cream
* 1½ cups semi-sweet chocolate chips

Ganache Ingredients
* 6 oz. semi-sweet chocolate, finely chopped
* 2 Tablespoons unsalted butter
* ½ cup heavy cream

Prepare

Preheat oven to 325 degrees. Have all ingredients at room temperature. Grease the Bundt cake pan and dust with cocoa powder. Tap out excess.

Make the Cake

In a bowl, combine the 1 cup of cocoa powder and the semi-sweet chocolate. Add the boiling water and whisk until the chocolate melts and the mixture is smooth and blended. Set aside.

Over a sheet of parchment paper, sift together the flour, baking soda, and salt. Set aside.

In your Kitchen Aid or a large bowl, beat the butter on medium speed until smooth and creamy, 30 to 45 seconds. Reduce the speed to low, add the brown sugar, and beat until blended. Increase the speed to medium and continue beating until the mixture is light and fluffy, about 5 minutes. Stop the mixer occasionally to scrape down the sides of the bowl. Add the beaten eggs a little bit at a time, beating until incorporated before adding more. Beat in the vanilla until incorporated, about 1 minute.

Reduce the speed to low and add the flour mixture in three additions. Alternate adding flour with adding sour cream and begin and end with the flour. Beat just until blended and no lumps of flour remain. Slowly pour in the chocolate-cocoa mixture and beat until no white streaks are visible. Stop the mixer occasionally to scrap down the sides of the bowl. Using a rubber spatula, gently fold in the chocolate chips.

Pour the batter into the prepared pan, spreading the batter so the sides are about 1 inch higher than the center. Bake until a toothpick inserted into the center of the cake comes out with only a few moist crumbs attached to it, 60 to 65 minutes. Transfer the pan to a wire rack and let the cake cool upright in the pan for 15 minutes. Invert the pan onto the rack and lift off the pan. Let the cake cool completely, at least 1 hour.

Return the cooled cake to the pan. Using a serrated knife, gently saw off any excess cake that extends over the edge of the pan. Set the wire rack on a parchment-lined baking sheet. Invert the pan onto the rack and lift off pan.

Make the Ganache

In a heat-proof bowl, combine the chocolate and butter. In a small saucepan over medium-high heat, bring the cream just to a boil. Immediately pour the cream over the chocolate and butter. Whisk until they melt and the mixture is smooth. Pour the ganache over the top of the cake, allowing the ganache to drip down the sides. Let the cake stand until the ganache is set, at least 15 minutes. Serves 16.

Aunt Patti's Lemon Bundt Cake

According to my sister Patti, she made this cake for special Sunday dinners while her children were growing up and when they were home from college. Her kids (now very much adults) loved this cake and couldn't get enough of it. So here it is for all your little kids (and big kids too).

Topping
- 2 Tablespoons butter, melted
- ½ cup chopped pecans
- ½ cup flaked coconut

Cake Ingredients
- 1 box moist lemon cake mix
- 8 oz. light sour cream
- 4 eggs
- ¼ cup water
- 2 Tablespoons vegetable oil
- Zest of one fresh lemon
- 1 teaspoon lemon extract (optional)

Glaze Ingredients
- 1 cup confectioners' sugar
- 2 Tablespoons lemon juice

Make the Topping (or the Bottoming)

Preheat oven to 350 degrees. Mix together melted butter, chopped pecans, and coconut. Spread this evenly in the bottom of a Bundt pan.

Make the Cake

In your Kitchen Aid or a large bowl, combine all cake ingredients and beat together on medium speed until well blended, about 2 to 3 minutes. Spoon batter into Bundt pan over the coconut-nut mixture.

Bake the Cake

Bake at 350 degrees for 45 to 50 minutes. The cake is done when it looks golden brown and bounces or when a toothpick comes out clean. Let cool and turn out onto fancy cake plate.

Make the Glaze

Mix together confectioners' sugar and lemon juice. Beat until smooth and drizzle over cooled cake.

Red Velvet Valentine's Cake

For Valentines Day or any day you want to evoke a little romance or just let the kids know you love them, make this cake. It is not only deliciously chocolate; it is heart-shaped and red—really red.

Cake Ingredients
- 2 ounces red food coloring
- 3 Tablespoons instant cocoa powder
- ½ cup butter
- 1½ cups sugar
- 2 eggs
- 1 cup buttermilk
- 2¼ cups cake flour
- 1 teaspoon salt
- 1 teaspoon vanilla
- 1 Tablespoon vinegar
- 1 teaspoon baking soda

Frosting Ingredients
- 1 large (8 ounce) package cream cheese, softened
- 1 box powdered sugar
- 1 cup milk
- 1 teaspoon vanilla
- ½ cup shredded coconut (optional)

Prepare

Preheat the oven to 350 degrees. Grease one 8" x 8" square cake pan and one 8" round cake pan.

Make Cake

In a small bowl, mix food coloring and cocoa to make a food coloring paste. Set aside. In your Kitchen Aid or large bowl, cream together butter and sugar. Add eggs and food coloring paste. Beat 10 minutes. Add buttermilk and slowly add flour. Add salt and vanilla. In a separate bowl, mix together vinegar and baking soda, then add to batter. Spoon batter into cake pans. Bake at 350 degrees for 30 to 35 minutes. Let cool.

Make Frosting

Soften the cream cheese in a bowl. Add powdered sugar alternating with milk as needed until you get the consistency for frosting. You may not need the whole box of powdered sugar or the whole cup of milk. Add vanilla. If you want pink frosting, add a little of the red food coloring to the frosting.

Assemble

Cut the round cake in half. Put the square cake on a cake serving platter and turn so the square is a diamond shape. Put the two halves of the round cake up against the top sides of the diamond. This makes a heart shape. Frost the cake and sprinkle the coconut on top.

Sue's Whole Wheat Honey Hippie Cake

Back in the 1970's when all the women poured into the workplace in professional jobs, day care was nearly impossible to find. Many people used the next door neighbor. My next door neighbor was a wonderful earth mother, Sue. We both had darling little boys, and they played together well. I could always depend on her to feed my baby healthy food. Sue was my model for the perfect urban hippie mom. She gave me this very healthy cake.

Cake
- 2 cups whole wheat pastry flour
- 2 teaspoons baking powder
- ½ teaspoon salt
- ¾ cup honey
- 1 cup butter (2 sticks), softened
- 1 egg
- 1 cup yogurt
- 1 teaspoon vanilla
- ¼ cup raisins
- ¼ cup chopped nuts (optional)

Topping
- ¼ cup milk
- ¼ cup butter
- ½ cup chopped nuts
- ½ cup honey

Prepare
Preheat the oven to 350 degrees. Grease an 8" x 8" cake pan.

Make Cake
In your Kitchen Aid or a large mixing bowl, mix flour, baking powder, and salt. Add the honey. Cut in the butter with a pastry blender. In a separate small mixing bowl, beat the egg and add it to the flour mixture along with the yogurt and vanilla. Add nuts and raisins. Pour into greased cake pan.

Make Topping and Bake

In a small saucepan, bring milk, butter, and nuts to boil. Turn off heat, add honey, and mix well. Pour topping over cake before baking. Bake at 350 degrees for 30 minutes.

Dame Ina Pinkney's Chocolate Soufflé Cake

Ina Pinkney is a legend in the Chicago restaurant scene. Her West Loop restaurant, Ina's, is a major destination for brunch. She is so popular because she has recipes like this one. Here is what Ina says about this cake:

"When I first discovered the new genre of 'flourless' chocolate cakes in the 1980's, they were all deep, dark, and dense. I wondered if the cake could go 'butterless' as well! This turned out to be my all-time favorite. When my former husband, Captain Bill Pinkney, returned from his sail around the world, he told me that this was the only dessert he longed for. I made it on his first day home."

Cake
- 9 large eggs, separated, and at room temperature
- 1 cup confectioners' sugar
- ½ cup unsweetened cocoa powder
- 1 teaspoon vanilla
- ½ teaspoon cream of tartar

Frosting
- 2 cups cold heavy whipping cream
- ½ cup confectioners' sugar
- ¼ cup unsweetened cocoa powder
- White or dark chocolate shavings for garnish (optional)

Prepare
Preheat oven to 350 degrees. Line the bottom of a 9-inch springform pan with parchment paper. Butter or oil sides of pan.

Make Cake
In a medium bowl, combine the egg yolks, confectioners' sugar, and cocoa powder. Beat until thick and lightened in color. Stir in the vanilla. Set aside.

In your Kitchen Aid or a large mixing bowl, beat the egg whites until frothy. Large bubbles should appear around the edge. Add the cream of tartar and increase the mixing speed until the whites are thick and glossy. To test, tilt the bowl. If the whites slide, they need a little more beating. Gently fold a large spoonful of the beaten whites into the chocolate mixture to lighten it. Gently fold the remaining whites and the chocolate mixture together. Carefully spoon into prepared pan.

Bake Cake

Bake the cake at 350 degrees for 35 to 40 minutes. The cake will be rounded when removed from the oven and the center will sink as it cools. Remove springform pan. Cool completely on a wire rack.

Make Frosting

In a blender, whip the whipping cream into soft peaks. Add the confectioners' sugar and cocoa powder gradually continuing to whip the cream into stiff peaks.

Frost

Place a flat plate on top of the cake. Turn cake over so the flat bottom is now on top. Remove parchment paper. Frost top of cake with a spatula.

Purist Hippie Carrot Cake

I've included this cake for historical purposes only. Unless you are into totally natural, don't really make this cake. Or make this cake and frost it with the cream cheese frosting described in the *Aunt Jane's Carrot Cake with Fruit* recipe that follows.

You may or may not know that it was the hippies back in the day who introduced or reintroduced carrot cake to the American cooking scene. They thought that with all those actual, real carrots in the cake, it would at least provide some healthy sustenance for their kids when they craved sweets. I made it all the time when my son was a boy. And every time I made carrot cake, I would have scrapes on my knuckles from all that grating of the carrots down to the carrot nubs. But I always felt virtuous because:

- I made it from scratch rather than from a box.
- It was made with whole wheat flour and no sugar.
- It was sweetened with raisins, dates, and pure unsweetened apple sauce.
- It had all those good spices which were considered healthy for you.
- We did not frost it with sugary or cream cheese frosting.

In those days, the real purists were opposed to using any kind of white sugar, white flour, Crisco shortening, or oils high in saturated fats (We did not know about trans fats back then, but it turned out we were right about oils.). And some real purists would not use store-bought eggs. So you won't find any of those ingredients in this purist carrot cake. And it might taste a little strange.

My mother never heard of or made a carrot cake back in the 1950's. I don't even know if carrot cake existed before the health food-conscious hippies and back-to-the-landers started making it. Now, carrot cake is standard fare at every restaurant, coffee shop, and bakery in the U.S. For the most part, these revised cakes are made with white flour, eggs, oil, and refined sugar. The frosting is a high-calorie, cream cheese nightmare. You can't pretend that these newer versions are healthy. But, whether you make the purist version of the cake provided here or the newer versions, you are still getting some vegetables into you. Just another great thing that the hippies from the Baby Boom generation have contributed to American culture.

- ½ cup grated carrots
- 1¼ cups chopped dates
- 1 cup raisins
- 1¼ cups water
- ½ cup unsweetened applesauce
- 1 teaspoon cinnamon
- 1 teaspoon allspice
- ½ teaspoon nutmeg
- ¼ teaspoon cloves
- 2 cups whole wheat pastry flour
- 1 teaspoon baking powder
- 1 teaspoon baking soda

Preheat oven to 350 degrees. Oil and flour an 8' x 8" cake pan. In a medium saucepan, combine carrots, dates, raisins, water, applesauce, cinnamon, allspice, nutmeg, and cloves. Bring to a boil. Reduce heat and simmer for 5 minutes. Cool.

In a large bowl, mix together the flour, baking powder, and baking soda. Add the carrot mixture and stir just until mixed. Bake at 350 degrees for 45 to 50 minutes.

Non-Purist Frosting

If you don't mind just a little sugar, use a sifter or a small strainer to sprinkle confectioners' sugar over the top of the cooled cake.

Aunt Jane's Carrot Cake with Fruit

If you checked out the purist carrot cake recipe included in this section, and decided it was not for you, I have provided a more palatable, modern version here for you. This is a pretty standard carrot cake but with an added twist. The pineapple and coconut really make this unique. And you are getting both a fruit and a vegetable serving in one dessert. This cake is very moist and delicious and everyone loves it, even people that say they don't like cake.

Cake Ingredients
- 2 cups all-purpose flour
- 2 cups granulated sugar
- ½ teaspoon salt
- 1 teaspoon baking soda
- 2 teaspoon ground cinnamon
- ½ teaspoon ground nutmeg
- 3 eggs
- 1½ cups vegetable oil
- 2 cups finely grated carrots (about 3 to 4 medium carrots)
- 2 teaspoons vanilla
- 1 can (8 ounces) well drained crushed pineapple
- 1 cup shredded coconut
- ½ cup chopped walnuts or pecans
- Extra nuts to decorate top

Frosting Ingredients
- ½ cup butter, softened
- 1 pkg. (8 oz.) cream cheese, softened
- 1 teaspoon vanilla
- 1 lb. powdered sugar, sifted

Prepare
Preheat oven to 350 degrees. Grease and flour a 9" x 13" baking pan.

Make Batter

In a mixing bowl combine flour, sugar, salt, soda, cinnamon, and nutmeg. Stir to blend. Add eggs, oil, carrots, and vanilla. Beat until well blended. Drain pineapple well squeezing out juice with hands. Stir in pineapple, coconut, and nuts. Pour into greased and floured baking pan.

Bake

Bake at 350 degrees for 50 to 60 minutes or until a tooth pick inserted in center comes out clean. Place cake in pan on a rack to cool.

Make Frosting

Mix all the frosting ingredients together in medium bowl. Frost the cooled cake and sprinkle with remaining chopped nuts, pressing into the frosting very lightly.

Cousin Karin's Guinness Cake

Adapted from a recipe by Tish Boyle, The Cake Book, *Wiley, 2006.*

Here is a cake that will go over big on St. Patrick's Day or during football season. Make it for your Superbowl party or, what the heck, any sports event. And, of course, it uses the mother's milk of my family's Irish background – Guinness beer.

And cousin Courtney informs me that Guinness beer is great for bringing your milk up when breastfeeding. It is also one of the lowest carb beers on the market!

- ¾ cups all-purpose flour
- ¾ cup natural (not Dutch-processed) cocoa powder
- 1¾ teaspoons baking powder
- ½ teaspoon baking soda
- ½ teaspoon ground cinnamon
- 2 sticks plus 5 Tablespoons unsalted butter, softened
- 2¼ cups firmly packed light brown sugar
- 3 large eggs
- 1½ teaspoons vanilla
- 1½ cups Guinness stout (do not include foam when measuring)
- 1 cup coarsely chopped pecans

Prepare

Position a rack in the center of the oven and preheat the oven to 325 degrees. Grease the bottom and sides of a 9-inch round cake pan or springform pan. Dust the pan with flour.

Make the Cake

Sift together the flour, cocoa powder, baking powder, baking soda, and cinnamon in a medium bowl. Whisk to combine, and set aside.

In your Kitchen Aid using the paddle attachment, beat the butter at medium-high speed until creamy, about 1 minute. Gradually add the brown sugar and beat at high speed until very light and creamy, about 3 minutes. Reduce the speed to medium-low and add the eggs one at a time. Beat well after each addition and scrape down the sides of the bowl with a rubber spatula as necessary.

Beat in the vanilla. Reduce the speed to low and add the dry ingredients in three additions, alternating with the stout in two additions and mixing just until blended. Add the pecans and mix just until combined. Remove bowl from the mixer stand and stir a few times with the rubber spatula to make sure the batter is evenly blended. Scrape the batter into the prepared pan and smooth the top.

Bake the Cake

Be sure to put a cookie sheet under the cake while baking as it might overflow the top. Bake for 70 to 75 minutes, until a cake tester inserted into the center comes out clean. Cool the cake in the pan on a rack for 20 minutes. Invert the cake onto the rack and cool completely. Just before serving, dust the top of the cake lightly with confectioners' sugar. Store in an airtight container at room temperature for up to a week.

Pies and Tarts

✦

Uncle Dick's Best Pastry Dough

Making pastry dough is a real art. And uncle Dick makes the best crust I ever tasted. He can make it light, flakey, and golden brown around the edges every time. Consistency is the key, and it takes practice, special equipment, and a light touch.

The right equipment and the right temperatures at the right time are key to making perfect dough every time. If you plan to make more than two pies a year, it is worth it to invest in the special equipment necessary. Marble slabs and marble rolling pins are easy to find in any kitchen store, and they are important because they hold the cold. Cold is key when you are rolling and handling the dough. Everything near the dough needs to be cold. A pastry cutter and pastry lifter are pretty much required for any pastry making. If you follow all the tips in this recipe and practice, practice, practice, before long, you'll get to the Carnegie Hall of perfect dough.

Special Equipment
- Pastry cutter
- Marble rolling pin
- Marble rolling slab (if possible)
- Pastry lifter

Ingredients
- 1 cup flour
- 1 stick cold butter
- ¼ cup very cold water

Prepare
Butter a 9-inch pie pan, but do not flour. Use a marble rolling pin if you can, and put it in the freezer now.

Make the Dough
Cut the cold butter into flour with a pastry cutter or two knives till the butter is smaller than pea-sized. Add cold water and form the dough into a ball with your fingers. Cut dough into one larger ball for bottom crust and

one slightly smaller ball for top crust. Try to handle the dough as little as possible while forming into balls. Chill two dough balls for one full hour.

Roll the Dough

Remove the marble rolling pin from the refrigerator and give it a light dusting with flour. Roll out the two crusts on a cold marble slab covered with a dusting of flour. While rolling, use a pastry lifter to assure that the dough does not stick to the slab. For a 9-inch 2-crust pie, roll the bottom crust to a 12-inch diameter. Roll the top crust to a 10" diameter.

Fold and Place Bottom Crust

To move the bottom crust into the pie pan, fold the crust in half and in half again. Using the pastry lifter, lift gently into one quarter of the pie pan. Unfold carefully. You should have one or two-inches of crust falling over the edge of the pie pan.

Fold and Place the Top Crust

After you put the filling into the bottom crust, place the top crust carefully over the contents using the same method you used for the bottom crust. Always cut steam holes in a top crust or cut out leaves or other designs. For making lattice on the top of a pie, see *Aunt Alice's Prize-Winning Blueberry Pie with Lattice.*

Finish Edges

Cut off excess dough and press the top and bottom crusts together leaving a good amount of pressed dough sitting on top of the pan edge. Remove excess crust.

To make a nice presentation of the crust edge, hold the thumb and forefinger of your left hand about one inch apart and place the tips of these fingers on the edge of the pan. With your right forefinger press the dough in between the left hand configuration. Do this all around for a professional look.

Aunt Alice's Prize-Winning Blueberry Pie with Lattice

Although I always use this recipe for blueberry pie, you can also use it for any berry pie including blackberry or raspberry. The variation I like to use for berry pie is the tapioca dry variation rather than the more common cornstarch, fruit juice wet variation. Tapioca is a very good thickener, and I think it makes the pie taste better than those with that cornstarchy taste.

About Blueberries

Speaking of blueberries, I am partial to Michigan blueberries just because we, in Chicago, can get them very easily when they are at the peak of their freshness. They are so easy to freeze, so we buy a whole flat for about $10 at any berry-picking place in the southwest corner of Michigan.

To freeze fresh blueberries, first clean and wash. Then sort. When sorting, besides removing substandard berries, be sure to remove all stems. Spread as many blueberries as you can on a cookie sheet that has substantial sides. Put in the freezer overnight. I use several cookie sheets and just pile them one on top of the other. In the morning, remove berries from freezer and pack into large freezer bags. If you are planning to make pies at a later date, put 4 cups of blueberries in each freezer bag. Put these bags in the back of the freezer and pull them out in January. Leave bags to defrost, and put these luscious berries on your oatmeal, waffles, or pancakes. Voila, a little summer freshness in your mouth in the depth of winter. Or, just go ahead and make the best blueberry pie you'll ever eat.

About Lattice

To me, the lattice is the fun, creative part of this pie. Lattice is the woven look you see on professional, old-fashioned pies at some of the better bakeries. I always think that the look of the pie is as important to its scrumptiousness as the taste. I can assure you that you will impress any crowd, large or small, with a homemade, fancy lattice-topped pie. They will think you are Irma Rombauer herself or will encourage you to go on a TV reality show. And, it is not that difficult if you know the tips and tricks ahead of time, as are presented here.

Crust

- *Dick's Best Pastry Dough* pie crust for a two-crust pie

Filling

- 4 cups fresh, Michigan-picked blueberries (or any fresh blueberries)
- 2 2/3 Tablespoons quick-cooking tapioca
- 2/3 to 1 cup sugar
- 1½ Tablespoons lemon juice
- 1 to 2 Tablespoons butter cut into tiny squares

Prepare

Preheat the oven to 450 degrees. Take out one 9-inch pie pan. Make the two-crust pie crust described in *Dick's Best Pastry Dough*. You may want to separate the two dough balls into equal balls to assure enough dough for the lattice. While the crust is cooling in the refrigerator, start the blueberry filling. Clean fresh blueberries by picking out the hard and undersized berries and removing all stems, leaves, and other non-edible debris.

Mix the Filling

In a large bowl that will hold all the blueberries, mix together the tapioca and sugar. Throw in the cleaned blueberries and mix carefully with a wooden spoon or spatula. Be careful not to break the berries. Just mix gently to make sure all the berries are covered with tapioca and sugar. Let this mixture sit for 15 minutes. This is very important because this is how the berry juices are extracted from the berries while leaving the berries in tact. After the 15-minute waiting period, add the lemon juice and mix again carefully. Let sit.

Create the Lattice Strips

Remove the prepared pie crust from the refrigerator and let sit at room temperature until easily handleable. Roll out the first crust into a 10- or 11-inch round. Line the bottom of the pie pan with this crust. Leave the edge as is for now.

Roll out the second crust into an 11-inch round. Dust a sharp knife or a pastry pinking roller with flour. Now, you will cut the strips you need for weaving the lattice. You will need about 14 strips of all different lengths. Start in the middle and cut one 11-inch by ½-inch strip. On either side of that, cut two 9- to 10-inch by ½-inch strips. Continue cutting ½-inch strips of shorter and shorter length until you have a total of fourteen ½-inch wide strips.

That is the ideal scenario, but cutting strips is not always perfect. You may have broken strips because of dough quality or other problems. Don't worry. Cut as many good strips from the first roll-out as possible, reducing the length of strips to accommodate the roundness of the pie. Then take all the scraps and re-roll. Cut more strips as need from the new crust. Try not to re-roll more than once as the dough will get tough.

Weave the Lattice

Place the longest strip in the middle of the pie. Place two of the next longest strips on either side of the middle strip about ½-inch over, leaving the blueberry filling showing on either side. Continue placing strips about ½-inch from each other with the shortest strip on the edge of the pie pan. You should have about 7 strips on the pie. Now you are going to weave the crust. See picture below for visual guide.

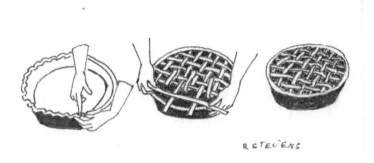

R STEVENS

Have the additional 7 strips ready at hand. Starting at one end of the pie pan, fold back every other strip you have already placed on the pie to the halfway mark. Take the longest strip you have at the ready and place it on top of the remaining strips in the middle of the pie perpendicular to the original longest strip. Unfold the folded strips back over this strip. Now fold back the strips that were left flat to the halfway mark. Place the second longest strip ½-inch from the first strip and unfold the strips over this new strip. Repeat until you reach the end of the pan. Now do the same on the second half of the pie.

After the lattice has been woven, cut the butter into tiny squares and place a square in each hole in the lattice.

Cut off extra crust on the edges of the pie, and pinch the crust to create a fat even edge all around. With your thumb and forefinger on one hand held slightly apart on the edge of the pie pan, push the crust between them with the forefinger of your other hand. This makes a nice professional-looking edge.

Finish

Place the pie in the oven equidistance from the top and bottom with a cookie sheet under it to catch the dripping filling. Bake for 10 minute at 450 degrees to brown the crust. Depending on your oven, you may want to watch the pie crust edges the first time you bake it to make sure that these edges do not burn. Adjust the baking time to avoid this. After the first 10 minutes, reduce the heat to 350 degrees and bake for 40 to 45 minutes.

Gourmet Banana-Cream Pie

Adapted from The New York Times Magazine *1/14/07*.

I have cut out the crème fraiche and the vanilla bean from this New York Times version of this very good pie. Who can get crème fraiche easily in the U.S. today? Although I know many purists would not think whipped cream could be substituted for crème fresh, I would for this dessert. My take on whipped cream topping is to go out and get the high-end brand of ready-made whipped cream and squirt it on just before you serve the pie. Or if you really want totally fresh, you can buy whipping cream and whip it up to hard peaks with your Kitchen Aid.

This recipe also includes a standard, home-made graham cracker crust—a good moist one. This is to counteract the current practice of buying those dry-ass, store-bought graham-cracker crusts. I made that mistake once and almost lost a husband. This is the real thing. I know this rant sounds like I am contradicting myself for buying the ready-made whipped cream and not the store-bought crust. Whatever!

Graham-Cracker Crust
- 1¼ cups graham-cracker crumbs (about 10 whole crackers)
- 1 teaspoon sugar
- 4 Tablespoons butter, melted

Pastry Cream
- 1 2/3 cups milk
- ¼ cup plus 3 Tablespoons sugar
- 1 teaspoon vanilla
- 3 Tablespoons cornstarch
- 1 large egg
- 2 large egg yolks
- 1½ Tablespoons butter
- ½ cup whipped cream
- 1½ medium bananas, sliced into 3/8-inch thick rounds

Assembly
- 2 medium bananas, sliced into 3/8-inch thick rounds
- Whipped cream

Make the Crust
Preheat oven to 325 degrees. In a medium sized bowl, combine the crumbs and sugar. Add the butter and mix, first with a fork, then with your fingers, until the crumbs are moistened. Pat the crumb mixture into a 9-inch pie pan, using your fingers and palm to press the crumbs evenly. The edges of the shell will be crumbly. Bake until lightly browned, about 9 to 10 minutes. Cool completely.

Make the Pastry Cream
In a medium saucepan over medium heat, combine the milk, ¼ cup sugar, and vanilla and bring to a simmer. In a separate small bowl, mix the remaining 3 tablespoons of sugar with the cornstarch. In yet another bowl, whisk together the egg and yolks. Add the cornstarch mixture to the eggs, and whisk until well combined. While whisking the egg mixture, slowly pour in about ¼ of the milk from the saucepan. Transfer this mixture into the saucepan, set over low heat and simmer, whisking constantly until it reaches the consistency of thick pudding. (Be careful not to curdle the eggs.) Remove from the heat and stir in the butter until incorporated. Pour into a shallow bowl or glass pie pan. Place plastic wrap directly over the surface, and chill for about 1 hour. After the pastry cream has cooled, remove the plastic, transfer it to a large bowl, and whisk until smooth. Fold in ½ cup of whipped cream and 1½ bananas cut into 3/8-inch rounds.

Assemble the Pie
Line the bottom of the cooled pie shell with a layer of banana slices. Pour the pastry cream over the top of the bananas. Squirt whipped cream over the pastry cream, covering the whole pie. Serve immediately.

Store the Pie and Serve the Next Day
If possible, serve the pie the next day. The banana taste is much more intense and the whole pie is more integrated after a day's storage. If you plan to wait, don't put the whipped cream on until just before you serve the pie. Instead, store the pie in the refrigerator. To keep the pastry cream fresh, cover it with saran wrap. When you are ready to serve the pie, squirt on the whipped cream over the whole pie and serve. Serves 8.

Sweet Potato Pie

This is a great pie to make in the fall or for Thanksgiving. It doesn't have to take the place of the pumpkin pie. You can make both since this one is so easy. You cook sweet potatoes just like regular potatoes, but don't try to peal these before you cook them. The skins come off so easily after they are cooked. Just boil them for 20 minutes of so until you can stick a fork through the tough skin and the inside feels soft. When you drain and peel them, the skins fall off for the most part. Just flick them off with a knife if they stick to the potato.

Sweet potatoes are supposed to possess miraculously wonderful healing powers since they contain all kinds of good things. This is one of the staples of the macrobiotic diet. Forget the macrobiotic diet, but do bake and eat sweet potatoes. Sweet potatoes are otherwise known as yams. This recipe makes two one-crust pies.

- Pastry crusts prepared in two pie pans (See *Dick's Best Pastry Dough*)
- 4 cups of cooked, soft sweet potatoes
- ½ cup butter (one stick)
- 2 cups sugar
- 1 teaspoon vanilla
- Nutmeg to taste
- 1 can of evaporated milk
- 3 eggs

Cook the sweet potatoes and prepare the pastry crusts in two pie pans. Preheat the oven to 350 degrees. Mix all ingredients together in the order listed. Pour into the prepared pastry crusts. Bake at 350 degrees for 1 hour.

Spicy Peach Tart

Variation on Spicy Pear Tart in The New Irish Table: 70 Contemporary Recipes, *Margaret M. Johnson, Chronicle Books LLC, San Francisco, 2003.*

I have made this recipe countless times for special occasions or just because the peaches were so good that year. You can also make this with pears. But the pears have to be just perfectly ripe and able to stand up to a lot of handling. This is true of the peaches also, but peaches seem to be much more available in a ripe state more often during the year than pears. I make this for Christmas Eve dinner every year. Look for peaches in the winter in a gourmet grocery.

One of the delightful things about this tart is that it looks beautiful and professional. All you need to look like a gourmet pastry chef is to buy a good 10-inch springform pan or a standard French tart pan where the bottom is removable. I prefer the tart pan as it is just easier to handle with this delicate tart. It is not difficult to make. It takes about 25 minutes to prepare and just over an hour to cook. And it's always a big hit. Three really important tips:

1. Take seriously the lining of the pan with double aluminum. You do not want this to leak.
2. Don't burn the caramel. Stir constantly to keep it from hardening on the bottom of the pan. When it starts bubbling softly, remove from heat.
3. Be sure to use superfine rather than regular sugar. It really gives it a fine, professional touch.

Caramel Crust
- 1 cup packed light brown sugar
- ½ cup (1 stick) unsalted butter

Batter
- 1½ cups flour
- 1 cup superfine sugar
- 1 teaspoon baking powder
- 1 teaspoon ground ginger

- 2 teaspoons ground cinnamon
- ½ teaspoon salt
- 2 eggs
- 2/3 cups canola oil
- 1 peach, peeled, cored, and shredded

Top
- 3 or 4 peaches (or pears), peeled and cored

Prepare
Preheat the oven to 300 degrees. Wrap a 10-inch springform pan or removable bottom tart pan in two layers of aluminum foil to prevent leaking. Butter the aluminum foil.

Make Crust
In a small saucepan, combine the brown sugar and butter over medium heat. Cook stirring constantly for about five minutes until the butter and sugar caramelize. Pour the caramel into the prepared tart pan and set aside to cool and harden.

Make Batter
Using the large holes of a box grater, shred one peach. In a medium bowl combine the flour, superfine sugar, baking powder, ginger, cinnamon, and salt. In a separate larger bowl, beat the eggs and oil together and add the shredded peach. Stir the dry ingredients into the egg mixture. Pour the batter over the caramel base in the tart pan.

Prepare and Arrange Top
Slice the remaining peaches. The fruit needs to be ripe but not sloppy. You will need to handle each slice at least twice. Slice the fruit as thin as possible. You need a lot of slices to cover the whole top of the tart. I have used three whole medium-sized peaches and found that to be enough, but just to be sure, you may want to slice up to four peaches. Sort small slices from larger slices. Starting in the center with the small ones, arrange the slices on top of the batter in concentric circles. Cover the batter entirely with slices.

Bake the Tart
Bake at 300 degrees for 1 hour and 15 minutes or until the base bubbles and the peaches turn soft. Remove from the oven and let cool slightly in the pan. Remove the sides of the pan. Move to a cake server plate. Slice and serve with whipped cream or ice cream. Serves 8 to 10.

Miscellaneous Goodies

✦

Chicago Hyde Park Chocolate Sauce

My son Chris' Grandma Edie on the Skeens side made the best chocolate sauce I've ever had, and it just so happens to be the same recipe that Chris' Grandpa Jim on the Stevens side made. Since both these grandpeople lived in Hyde Park on Chicago's south side, I am calling this Chicago Hyde Park Chocolate Sauce. But whatever, it is really great on vanilla or butter pecan ice cream.

It was always a special occasion when either of these grandparents made this delicious treat. Grandpa Jim had a special secret that he did reveal before his death in 2003. It's the kind of pan you use. Grandpa Jim used a small, heavy-bottomed, cast-iron enamel, La Creuset pan with a handle. He would not make the sauce without that pan.

Always make this sauce right before you serve it so it is hot and fresh. Grandpa Jim always made this sauce right after he finished dinner and not a minute before.

- ½ cup water
- 2 one-ounce squares of baking chocolate
- 1 ½ to 2 cups sugar
- 1 teaspoon butter

In a heavy saucepan over low heat, add the water and chocolate. Add 1½ cups sugar and cook slowly stirring constantly. When thickened, add the butter and stir until incorporated. If it does not thicken, add the ½ cup more of sugar. Serve hot over ice cream or any appropriate dessert.

Pumpkin and Spice Crème Brulee

Adapted from Elegantly Easy Crème Brulee, *Debbie Puente. Renaissance Books, 1998.*

This is a delicious and sophisticated alternative to pumpkin pie at Thanksgiving. It is light but rich and just the right amount to top off a great Thanksgiving meal when no one thinks they possibly have room for dessert. Serve this with a spoon, and, for those guests who may never have had crème brulee, make sure you let everyone know that they need to poke the spoon through to break the sugar-glazed top.

You will need to plan ahead when making this recipe because it requires 2 hours too cool, or you can let it cool in the refrigerator overnight. This is good for Thanksgiving because it is a dessert you can make ahead to avoid the bother on Thanksgiving Day.

Special Equipment
- Six four-ounce ramekins
- Butane torch or broiler

Ingredients
- 2 cups heavy cream
- 2 teaspoons vanilla
- 8 egg yolks
- 1/3 cup granulated sugar
- 1 cup pumpkin puree
- ¼ teaspoon ground cinnamon
- 1/8 teaspoon ground nutmeg
- ¼ teaspoon ground ginger
- ¼ cup granulated sugar for glazing the tops

Preheat the oven to 300 degrees. In a large bowl, whisk together the cream, vanilla, yolks, sugar, pumpkin, cinnamon, nutmeg, and ginger. Blend well. Divide mixture among six ramekins or custard cups.

Place in a water bath. A water bath is the equivalent of a double broiler in the oven. Place the custard-filled ramekins in a low pan, and place on the center rack of the oven. Carefully fill the pan with warm water until the level reaches halfway up the sides of the ramekins. Bake at 300 degrees until set around the edges, but still loose in the center, about 30 to 40 minutes. Remove from the oven and leave in the water bath until cooled. Remove cooled cups from water bath and chill for at least 2 hours or overnight.

When ready to serve, sprinkle about 2 teaspoons of sugar over each custard. Using a torch, caramelize the sugar until a hard top forms on the custard. Or set the cups under a broiler for a minute or two. Watch carefully. After caramelizing, re-chill custards for a few minutes before serving. Serves 6.

Traditional Chex Party Mix

Adapted from Chex Party Mix recipe of the Checkerboard Kitchens of the Ralston Purina Company, 1990.

Everyone needs this recipe at least once in their lives. And, from my experience, the recipe never seems to be around where you can find it when you need it. So here it is in your trusty goodies cookbook. You will need it for pre-teen or teen parties, a casual snack for a summer barbecue, or just for Saturday night when you are stuck home with the kids watching a movie. This updated version also gives you the microwave directions. Whoo Hoo!

- 6 Tablespoons butter
- 1½ teaspoons seasoned salt
- ¾ teaspoon garlic powder
- ½ teaspoon onion powder
- 2 Tablespoons Worcestershire sauce
- 3 cups Corn Chex
- 3 cups Rice Chex
- 3 cups Wheat Chex
- 1 cup salted peanuts or other nuts
- 1 cup Snyder's butter pretzels, broken into bite-sized pieces

Oven Baking

Preheat oven to 250 degrees. In an open roasting pan, melt the butter in the oven. In medium-sized bowl, mix seasoned salt, garlic powder, onion powder, and Worcestershire sauce. Add this to the butter in the oven. Gradually add cereals, nuts, and pretzels, stirring until all pieces are evenly coated. Bake 1 hour, stirring every 15 minutes. Spread on absorbent paper to cool. Store in airtight container.

Microwave

In a large microwave-safe bowl, melt the butter on high for 1 minute or until melted. Stir in the seasoned salt, garlic powder, onion powder, and Worcestershire sauce. Gradually add cereals, nuts, and pretzels, stirring until all pieces are evenly coated. Microwave on high for 5 to 6 minutes, stirring every 2 minutes. Spread on absorbent paper to cool. Store in airtight container. Makes 9 cups.

Aunt Mary's Chocolate Almond Tapioca Pudding

This is an unbelievably delicious variation on traditional tapioca pudding. The idea here is to make something more tasty with less sugar. Also, I replace the vanilla from the standard recipe with almond extract and add cocoa powder.

Let me just say, I have a hard time waiting for this recipe to cool. Although it makes six one-half cup servings, I find I eat the whole recipe myself in one big serving. So, I recommend that you at least double or triple this if you are serving others.

This recipe allows you to experiment. You can make tapioca with soy, coconut, two-percent, whole, fat-free, or lactose-free milk. Coconut milk and chocolate are a fabulous combination. Or put coconut on top of the pudding before or after cooling. Try bananas on top, or substitute rum extract for the almond extract. Add cinnamon. Be creative.

- 2½ cups milk
- 4 Tablespoons sugar, divided
- 3 Tablespoons tapioca
- 3 Tablespoons cocoa powder
- 1 egg white whipped to soft peaks
- 1 egg yolk
- 1¼ teaspoon almond extract

Prepare

Separate the egg. Whip the egg white with half the sugar (2 tablespoons) to soft peaks.

Cook the Pudding

In a medium saucepan, mix the milk, 2 tablespoons sugar, tapioca, and cocoa together and let sit 5 minutes. The tapioca needs to soften, so don't skip this resting period. Over medium heat, stir constantly until mixture comes to a full boil (a boil that doesn't stop boiling when stirred). Remove pan from heat. Fold in the egg white mixture immediately. Stir in almond extract. Cool thoroughly for at least 20 minutes. Pudding will thicken as it cools.

Serve and Store

Serve warm or chilled. To chill, refrigerate for two hours or overnight. For creamier pudding, place plastic wrap on surface of pudding before cooling Makes six, half-cup servings.

Jane's Rice Pudding

Jane Kohler was a veterinarian, a good friend, and a delightful roommate back in the day (1970s). She was thin as a rail and once said to me "You cannot eat the standard American three meals a day and stay slim." Well she was right about that, and she stayed thin. The last time I saw her she was on her way to Johns Hopkins to do research on how animal diseases can be transmitted to humans. I have no idea how all this relates to the rice pudding, but I love this rice pudding and you will too.

- 2 cups cooked white rice
- ½ cup water
- 2 cups milk
- ½ cup raisins
- 2 eggs
- ½ cup honey
- 1 teaspoon vanilla

In a large sauce pan cook the rice in the water. Simmer until all water is absorbed. Add milk and boil gently, stirring for 5 minutes until the mixture is thick. In a small bowl, beat the eggs, honey, and vanilla together. Slowly add this to the milk mixture, stirring constantly. Add the raisins and pour mixture into a casserole dish. Set casserole dish in a shallow pan filled with 1 inch of water. Bake at 350 for 30 to 40 minutes.

Printed in the United States
129124LV00004B/6/P

9 780595 526895